Cas Clarke is a careers officer who wrote her first book, *Grub on a Grant*, after taking a degree in Urban Studies at Sussex University. She now lives in a rural retreat in Surrey with her husband and their mad cat and dog, Matti and Barney. She was encouraged to write *Peckish but Poor* by the many fans of *Grub on a Grant* who felt it was time to move up a culinary step.

Also by Cas Clarke

Grub on a Grant

Peckish but Poor

Cas Clarke

HEADLINE

For my long-suffering husband,
Andy, with love

First published in 1993
by HEADLINE BOOK PUBLISHING PLC

10 9 8 7 6 5 4 3 2

ISBN 0 7472 3937 1

Typeset by
Letterpart Limited, Reigate, Surrey

Printed and bound in Great Britain by
HarperCollins Manufacturing, Glasgow

HEADLINE BOOK PUBLISHING
A division of Hodder Headline PLC
338 Euston Road
London NW1 3BH

Contents

Introduction

What do you do on that first day when you have left the comforts of home behind you and the only thing between you and starvation is an unknown kitchen with its hidden mysteries? Remember that well known phrase: 'Don't panic'. Those hidden mysteries can be all easily unravelled and soon you will discover the hidden pleasures of the kitchen. There is no need to resort to expensive pre-packaged meals or takeaways – these have a place in our lives but are too costly to feature frequently when living on a budget.

Many of us now leave home with little or no idea of how to prepare and cook simple meals, although this is a basic skill essential for our well-being and one that is not particularly hard to acquire. I hope that in this book I can show you how easy it is to cook tasty, nutritious yet inexpensive meals which you will enjoy both cooking and eating.

I can assure you that I am no Cordon Bleu cook, my only qualification being an old-fashioned O-Level in cookery! However, I do enjoy cooking and ever since leaving home I have experimented with new recipes. I am also incredibly lazy so I am always looking for simpler, quicker ways of doing things.

When deciding how to organise this book, I quickly came to the conclusion that the best way would be to gather together recipes that use seasonal produce. Therefore I have grouped recipes under the titles of Spring, Summer, Autumn and Winter. This may seem quite an old-fashioned way of putting a cookery book together, as with the advent of new varieties and distribution networks, most types of produce are now available all year round. However, there is a world of difference between the price of a strawberry in summer, when it is in season, and its price in winter when it has been expensively imported! Therefore, since this is a cookery book for people who are money-minded, I decided that it would be a good idea to relegate recipes using seasonal produce to the seasons when they are cheapest and, incidentally, when they are often at their tastiest.

I have added chapters on preparing and cooking vegetables and also on making desserts and cakes. As this is a book for people with limited budgets, I have also explained some of the basics in cookery that can save you money, for instance you can buy items such as stocks and pastry, but you can save money by making these items yourself. There is also a chapter on store-cupboard cookery, either for when you didn't make it to the shops or just need to conjure up one more meal out of thin air to make it through to pay day! Lastly my favourite chapter, Just Like Mother Used to Make . . . which is a collection of recipes to stop you feeling homesick – go on, spoil yourself!

Handy Hints

- The recipes in this book are generally for 2 people. This is because I have found that most of my friends have only really started taking an interest in cooking when they have finally settled down with a spouse or live-in lover. However, it is very easy to halve the ingredients if you are cooking for one, or double them if you have friends coming round. A few of the recipes are for 4 servings – this is because these recipes are very good eaten cold as well as hot and can therefore be served the next day too. In a few cases I suggest using 2 servings as a basis for another meal, e.g. my recipe for chilli con carne is for 4 servings, so you could have chilli con carne one day and then use the rest of the chilli in my recipe for chilli beef pie.

- Quantities of seasonings are only given as a guide; you will soon learn how to adjust them to suit your own taste.

- Read the recipe CAREFULLY to ensure you understand it. Please pay attention to words such as 'gently simmer' – this means just that. If you go ahead and boil it, you will end up with a burnt pan and dried up food! Also watch out for grilling on a 'medium' heat. Again, if you grill on high, you will probably end up with a burnt offering, or worse, a flash fire.

- Throughout the book I have used a standard conversion of 1 oz = 25g. For liquid measurements I use 1 fl oz = 25ml. These are not exact equivalents, so use one set of measurements or the other. Another useful piece of information is that 3 teaspoons = 1 tablespoon. (If you are halving 1 teaspoon of something because you are cooking for one, just a sprinkling, or dash if it is a liquid, will be sufficient.)

- Ovens vary enormously but you will soon learn how yours behaves. If dishes are coming out overdone, turn the heat down by 10°C/25°F/Gas 1 whenever you cook, or similarly if dishes always take longer to cook than the recipe states, turn the heat up by the same amount.

Shopping
- If you live near a pick-your-own farm, do take full advantage of the savings you can make with

seasonal produce. (It's also a nice way of spending a sunny afternoon.)

- Wherever you live, you will hopefully have access to a market. Fruit and vegetables, particularly, will be better and cheaper bought here. Just beware of traders who try to palm off shoddy goods on you.

- When buying fresh produce make sure you bear in mind when it is going to be used. There's no point buying something for Friday's supper if it will go off by Wednesday. This applies equally to meat, fish or vegetables.

- Although supermarkets are generally more expensive to shop in, you can also get some real bargains. Watch out for special offers. Because supermarkets buy in bulk, they can often offer discount prices.

- The other way of saving when using supermarkets is to shop late on Saturday afternoon. Fresh products are often marked down considerably, especially on items such as fish (although this is changing as some supermarkets are now open on Sundays).

- Supermarkets often mark down more unusual vegetables such as fennel and jerusalem artichokes. This happens because only a few people buy these (because they're different!) so it's a good way of obtaining vegetables which otherwise you could not afford on a limited budget.

Kitchen Utensils

You may have some kitchen utensils or you may be in the process of starting to stock your new home. These are my suggestions for what will come in handiest.

A couple of large **chopping boards** – it is best to keep one solely for cutting up meats.

Some good **sharp knives**. The most indispensable are a large chopping knife, a bread knife and a small knife with a serrated edge.

A couple of **medium saucepans with tight fitting lids**. It's a good idea to get a **steamer** which will fit one of these pans.

A small **saucepan/milkpan** for making sauces.

A large **frying pan or wok**.

You will need some ovenproof dishes – I suggest a **casserole dish with tight fitting lid**, a **gratin dish** and a **lasagne dish**, although if you can only afford one buy the lasagne dish.

Other bakeware should include a **baking tray**, 11 × 7 in (28 × 18 cm) **baking dish**, 8 in (20 cm) **flan tin**, 8 in (20 cm) **pie plate**, and for cakes 8 in (20 cm) **cake tins** and an 8 in (20 cm) **deep cake tin**. These should all be non stick to keep life simple.

You can never have too many **wooden spoons**.

If you don't have a steamer, you will need a **colander**.

A **swivel-bladed potato peeler** is quick to use.

You will also need a **sieve**.

A **rolling pin** will be needed for pastry.

Absolute essentials in my book are a pair of **kitchen scales**, **measuring jug**, and **measuring spoons**.

For making cakes I would also say that an **electric beater** is essential, it really makes a huge difference to the amount of work you have to put in. If, however, you don't have one, you will also need a **whisk**.

Ingredients

It seems that every week now new products become available to us. In compiling this book I have kept to a lot of ingredients which are readily available everywhere. However, where I have used some seasonings which not everyone will be able to obtain, they can generally be substituted with more common ingredients such as chilli or curry powder; use whatever YOU feel like using.

Here are my suggestions for items which you should keep in stock:

A couple of oils; my favourites are **olive oil** and **groundnut oil**. I always use **free-range eggs**, and, since I use a lot of garlic, I buy a **string of garlic** and keep it hanging on the wall. I love **butter** but also use a **low-fat soft sunflower margarine** which is suitable for baking. I keep both **self-raising** and **plain flour**, and a variety of sugars, the most commonly used ones being **soft brown**, **caster sugar** and **demerara**. It is useful to have a range of **pasta** and some **Parmesan cheese**. I tend to use a lot of **pesto**, **tomato purée** and **canned chopped tomatoes**.

I do use a lot of herbs and spices but I think you can get by with **Italian herbs**, **mixed herbs**, **paprika**, **chilli powder** and a medium **curry paste**. **Soy sauce** is essential and I also use a lot of **sweet chilli sauce**. I often use **runny honey**. And last, but certainly not least, you will always find some **tomato ketchup** in my fridge!

1 Down to Basics

If you take the time to learn and master certain basics, you can certainly save yourself a few pennies in your cookery. However, they are not essential. It is always possible to buy these items if necessary – but if you are really trying to keep your costs down, it would be well worth your while starting out here.

Stock
Makes 1 pint (500ml)

> meat or chicken bones
> 1 onion, chopped
> 1 carrot, diced
> bouquet garni
> 2 pints (1 litre) water

Put all ingredients in a large saucepan, bring to the boil and then simmer very gently until liquid is reduced by half. At this point strain through a fine sieve and leave to cool. As the liquid cools you will find that any fat floats to the top and can be skimmed off. The stock can now be used or, for a stronger base (for sauces, etc.), you can further reduce it by half.

Gravy
Makes 10 fl oz (250ml)

> 1 oz (25g) butter or meat fat
> 1 oz (25g) flour, sifted
> few drops gravy browning
> 10 fl oz (250ml) meat stock

Melt the butter or dripping and remove from heat, add flour and stir quickly. Add the gravy browning and a little stock, keep stirring. Return to heat and whilst stirring gradually add the remaining stock. When all stock has been incorporated continue cooking for 2 minutes.

White Sauce
Makes 10 fl oz (250ml)

> 1 oz (25g) butter or margarine
> 1 oz (25g) flour, sifted
> 10 fl oz (250ml) milk

Melt the butter or margarine in a small saucepan and then take the pan away from the heat and add the flour, stir well and return to a gentle heat, stirring continuously. Add a little of the milk, and keep stirring to ensure lumps do not appear. The mixture will be very thick, keep thinning it gradually with the milk. When all of the milk has been incorporated, keep stirring and continue cooking for a minute or two to ensure that the flour is cooked through.

This sauce can be used in a number of ways, e.g.

CHEESE
Add 2 oz (50g) grated cheese to the sauce and a touch of mustard.

PARSLEY
Add 2 tablespoons (30ml) chopped fresh parsley, with salt and pepper to taste.

MUSHROOM
Add 4 oz (100g) sliced mushrooms and 1 tablespoon (15ml) double cream.

Add the various extra ingredients when all the milk has been incorporated.

Tomato Sauce
Makes 10 fl oz (250ml)

oil for frying
1 garlic clove, chopped or crushed
14-oz (400-g) can chopped tomatoes
1 tablespoon (15ml) tomato purée
sprinkling of basil

Fry the garlic gently in the oil (if you can afford it, olive oil is the preferred oil for this dish). Add the rest of the ingredients and simmer very gently until the sauce is of the consistency that you want.

Garlic Bread

1 French baguette
4 oz (100g) softened butter
2 cloves garlic, crushed
1 tablespoon (15ml) fresh parsley, chopped

Cut the bread into thick slices without completely separating each slice. Cream the butter with the garlic and parsley, and use to spread on each sliced side. Wrap loosely in foil and bake in a pre-heated oven at 160°C/325°F/Gas 3 for 15 minutes. Fold foil back from bread, raise temperature to 220°C/425°F/Gas 7 and cook for a further 10 minutes or until crisp.

Pizza Dough
Makes 1 large pizza base

   4 oz (100g) strong white bread flour
   4 oz (100g) strong brown bread flour
   1 teaspoon (5ml) salt
   1 teaspoon (5ml) sugar
   1 teaspoon (5ml) easy-blend yeast
   1 teaspoon (5ml) olive oil
   5 fl oz (125ml) hand-hot water

Mix all ingredients together, then knead for 5 minutes. Leave the dough to rise in a covered bowl for 45 minutes. Before using knead once more until smooth. See p 154 for suggested toppings and cooking instructions.

Batter

   4 oz (100g) flour
   pinch of salt
   1 egg, beaten
   10 fl oz (250ml) milk

Put the flour and salt into a bowl. Make a well in the middle and put eggs and a little milk in this. Gradually beat liquid into flour. Add the rest of the milk a little at a time until you have a smooth batter. (Alternatively put everything into a blender and just whizz together.)

Shortcrust Pastry
Makes 12 oz (300g)

> 8 oz (200g) flour
> pinch of salt
> 5 oz (125g) butter, chopped
> cold water

Put the flour, salt and butter into a bowl. Using your fingertips rub the mixture between your fingers until it resembles fine breadcrumbs, then using a few tablespoons of water, mix to a dough. Only use as much water as is needed. Rest dough in fridge for 20 minutes before using. When rolling out, touch as little as possible and roll out on a floured surface using a rolling pin.

CHEESE PASTRY

Add 3 oz (75g) grated cheese and a egg yolk to the breadcrumb mixture. You will need barely any water to make this into a dough.

NUTTY PASTRY

Add 2 oz (50g) finely chopped nuts and an egg yolk to the breadcrumb mixture. Again, you will only need about 1 tablespoon (15ml) water to make this dough.

2 Spring

This time of the year is always unpredictable. When one thinks of springtime, the image that often comes to mind is one of blue skies and the garden springing into life. Unfortunately, however, it is just as likely to be wet and windy. Although lots of spring vegetables now start to appear in the shops, alongside home-produced, none of these are particularly cheap and will remain relatively expensive until the summer months. However, these are amongst the best months for fish and you should find that chicken is particularly cheap at this time of the year.

Because of the variable weather you may find yourself in the middle of a freak heatwave, when you will not want to spend time in the kitchen and will happily eat salad everyday, or the weather may be so miserable that you crave warming comfort food at the end of another wet and grey day. Therefore this is a chapter of mixed recipes so you can choose the foods to suit your and the weather's moods. But even if the rain does pour, remember, summer is just around the corner. . .

Honeyed Chicken
Serves 2

 4 chicken drumsticks
 1 teaspoon (5ml) paprika
 1 tablespoon (15ml) oil
 1 tablespoon (15ml) runny honey
 sprinkling of rosemary

Put the drumsticks in a foil tin or on a piece of baking foil (folded up slightly at the edges) then mix the paprika, oil and honey together and pour over the drumsticks. Sprinkle with the rosemary. Grill under a medium heat for 20 minutes, until cooked through (ie until only clear juices run out when prodded with a sharp knife). Baste occasionally with the juices and turn frequently so that both sides are cooked. Serve with new potatoes and either a green salad or vegetables.

Sausage and Potato Pie
Serves 2

Of course one always buys sausages by the pound. This means that whenever we have sausages for supper we have some left over. This recipe is ideal for using them up.

1 onion, sliced
knob of butter
4 cold cooked sausages
1 lb (400g) mashed potato or packet of mash, made up
4 oz (100g) cheese, grated
salt and pepper

Pre-heat oven to 190°C/375°F/Gas 5. Fry onion in butter until brown. Slice sausages into thick rounds. Pile onion and sausages into a greased pie dish. Mix mash and cheese and season well with salt and pepper. Spoon the mash mixture into the pie dish so that it covers the sausages. Even the surface of the mash with a fork. Bake for 40 minutes. Serve with baked or barbecued beans.

Frozen Fish Bake
Serves 2

12 oz (300g) any white frozen fish fillets
1 onion, chopped
1 clove garlic, crushed or chopped
knob of butter
8-oz (200-g) can chopped tomatoes
2 oz (50g) cheese, grated
sprinkling of rosemary

Pre-heat the oven to 200°C/400°F/Gas 6. Put the frozen fish fillets in a greased pie or casserole dish and bake for 10 minutes. Meanwhile fry the onion and garlic in the butter until brown, mix with the tomatoes and when the fish has been cooking for 10 minutes, mix the tomato and onion mixture into the fish. Cover with the cheese and sprinkle the rosemary over the top. Bake for 20–30 minutes until the fish is cooked and the cheese has melted and is starting to brown. Serve with new or baked potatoes and broccoli or cabbage.

Leek and Bacon Flan
Serves 4

3 lb (1.2kg) leeks, washed and sliced into rings
8 oz (200g) streaky bacon, rinded and diced
oil for frying
4 eggs, beaten
8 fl oz (200ml) single cream
salt and pepper
12 oz (300g) shortcrust pastry
4 oz (100g) cheese, grated

Pre-heat the oven to 190°C/375°F/Gas 5. Fry the leeks and
bacon in a little oil, until starting to brown, pour off any excess
oil and then mix with the eggs and cream, season with the salt
and pepper and leave to cool. Roll out the pastry until it will fit
into the bottom of a 7×11 in (18×28 cm) baking tray. Grease
the tray and lay the pastry in it. Prick well with a fork all over
the base. Spread the leek and bacon mixture evenly over the
pastry, sprinkle with the cheese. Cook for 30 minutes until the
mixture is risen and golden brown. Serve hot with baked
potatoes and baked beans or peas, or serve cold with new
potatoes and salad.

Mediterranean Gratin
Serves 2

    12 oz (300g) potatoes, cooked and sliced
    5 oz (125g) Mozzarella cheese, thinly sliced
    1 lb (400g) spinach, cleaned and cooked (or use frozen
        spinach)
    salt and pepper
    2 tablespoons (30ml) tomato purée
    3 tomatoes, sliced thinly
    2 eggs, beaten
    5 fl oz (125ml) single cream
    2 teaspoons (10ml) red pesto

Pre-heat the oven to 180°C/350°F/Gas 4. Into a greased casserole or lasagne dish put half of the potatoes, then half of the cheese, season the spinach with the salt and pepper and use to cover the cheese slices. Spread the tomato purée over the spinach. Cover with the remaining potato and then the sliced tomato. Mix together the egg, cream and red pesto, pour over the other ingredients and cook for 35–45 minutes, until top is golden. Serve with a green salad.

Baked Garlicky Chicken
Serves 2

2 chicken leg portions
1 onion, chopped
2 cloves garlic, chopped or crushed
1 tablespoon (15ml) oil
7-oz (200-g) can chopped tomatoes
squeeze of lemon juice
1 tablespoon (15ml) paprika
sprinkling of rosemary
black pepper
2 tablespoons (30ml) single cream

Pre-heat the oven to 180°C/350°F/Gas 4. Put the chicken pieces in a greased casserole dish. Fry the onion and garlic in the oil (use olive oil if you have it) until browning. Add the rest of ingredients except cream, mix well and then pour over the chicken. Cover tightly (using foil, if necessary, to get a really tight fit) and cook for 45–55 minutes until chicken is done (until juices run clear when prodded with a sharp knife). Just before serving, mix in the cream and sprinkle with a little more black pepper. Serve with rice and spinach salad, or new potatoes and broccoli.

Ham and Cheese Fry-up
Serves 2

4 freshly cut slices of bread
4 slices ham
4 slices Gruyère cheese
oil, for frying
4 slices tomato
chopped chives

Trim the ham and cheese to fit the bread slices. Fry the bread on one side until golden, turn bread over and add a slice of ham, cheese and then tomato to each slice of bread. Sprinkle with chives. Continue frying gently until bread has cooked and cheese is melting. Serve with a small salad garnish.

Honey and Ginger Glazed Chops
Serves 2

2 lamb or pork chops
1 teaspoon (5ml) ginger purée
1 teaspoon (5ml) wholegrain mustard
2 teaspoons (10ml) runny honey
1 clove garlic, crushed

Pre-heat the grill. Mix all seasonings and honey together, put chops under grill and cover with half the honey mixture. Cook under a medium heat for 5 minutes. Turn chops and cover with remaining honey mixture, grill again for a further 5 minutes. Serve with new potatoes and carrots.

Chickpea and Coriander Curry
Serves 2

1 onion, chopped
1 clove garlic, crushed or chopped
1 tablespoon (15ml) oil
1 oz (25g) creamed coconut
1 tablespoon (15ml) medium curry paste
14-oz (400-g) can chickpeas, drained
2 tablespoons (30ml) tomato purée
1 tablespoon (15ml) soft butter
fresh coriander leaves, shredded

Fry the onion and garlic in oil until browning. Make the creamed coconut into a soft paste with some hot water. Put all ingredients except coriander into a saucepan and heat gently, stirring continuously. When heated through, serve on a bed of rice, garnished with the coriander leaves.

Spiced Chicken
Serves 2

> 4 chicken drumsticks
> 1 tablespoon (15ml) Worcester sauce
> 1 teaspoon (5ml) paprika
> 1 tablespoon (15ml) tomato ketchup or barbecue sauce
> 1 tablespoon (15ml) runny honey

Mix the seasonings and honey together and then use to coat chicken. Mix thoroughly. Pre-heat the grill. Place the chicken in a foil tin or on a sheet of foil with the edges slightly turned up. Cook under a medium heat, turning frequently, for about 20 minutes or until chicken is cooked through and skin is turning crispy. Serve with new potatoes and salad.

Cod Steaks with Blue Cheese
Serves 2

> 2 × 6 oz (150g) cod steaks
> melted butter
> 2 oz (50g) Danish Blue cheese, crumbled

Pre-heat grill. Put cod on a buttered sheet of foil and brush with melted butter. Grill under a medium heat for 4 minutes. Turn steak over and brush with butter. Sprinkle with cheese. Grill for a further 4 minutes until fish is cooked and cheese has melted. Serve with new potatoes and peas, or jacket potato and salad.

Cajun Pork
Serves 2

> 2 pork chops
> 1 tablespoon (15ml) soft brown sugar
> 1 teaspoon (5ml) Cajun seasoning

Pre-heat the grill. Put the chops on the grill rack and sprinkle with some of the sugar and Cajun seasoning. Cook under a medium heat for 5 minutes until chops begin to glaze. Turn over and sprinkle with remaining sugar and seasoning, continue to cook for another 5 minutes until chops are cooked and well glazed. Serve with new potatoes and salad or rice mixed with cooked peas and sweetcorn.

Chicken and Mushroom Chow Mein
Serves 2

4 oz (100g) egg noodles
8 oz (200g) chicken breast, skinned and boned
4 oz (100g) mushrooms, sliced
1 tablespoon (15ml) oil
4 tablespoons (60ml) soy sauce
2 tablespoons (30ml) orange juice
1 teaspoon (5ml) cornflour
4 spring onions, chopped

Put the noodles in a bowl and cover with boiling water. Cut the chicken into bite-sized pieces. Fry chicken and mushrooms in oil for 4 minutes. Mix soy sauce, orange juice and cornflour together and add with spring onions to frying pan. Stir well. Drain noodles and add to pan. Cook until sauce is thickening. Serve immediately.

Stuffed Herring
Serves 2

2 herrings, filleted and heads removed
2 slices bread, crumbed
1 tablespoon (15ml) mixed nuts
4 oz (100g) mushrooms, finely chopped
knob of butter
2 teaspoons (10ml) tomato purée
1 tablespoon (15ml) cheese, grated

Make three shallow slits down each side of the fish. Put the herrings on a piece of foil, place on the grill rack and leave to one side. Pre-heat the grill. Quickly fry the breadcrumbs, nuts and mushrooms in the butter. When soft, remove from the heat and add the tomato purée and cheese, mix well. Use this mixture to stuff the herrings. Grill under a medium heat for 10 minutes and then turn fish over and grill for a further 10 minutes. Serve with new potatoes and a green vegetable.

Tagliatelle with Ham
Serves 2

> 6 oz (150g) tagliatelle
> 1 onion, chopped
> 1 clove garlic, chopped or crushed
> 2 oz (50g) butter
> 4 oz (100g) ham, chopped
> 2 oz (50g) cooked peas
> salt and pepper

Put tagliatelle on to cook (this should take approximately 8 minutes). Fry the onion and garlic in butter. When soft, add ham and peas. When tagliatelle is ready put into bowls, add the onion and ham, season well and serve immediately.

Coley with Spicy Sauce
Serves 2

> 2 × 6 oz (150g) coley fillets
> knob of butter
> 1 tablespoon (15ml) Worcester sauce
> 1 tablespoon (15ml) wholegrain mustard
> 1 tablespoon (15ml) tomato sauce

Fry fillets gently in butter for about 5 minutes on each side. Mix other ingredients together and, when fish is cooked, pour sauce over fish and allow to warm through. Serve with new potatoes and carrots.

Glazed Gammon Steaks
Serves 2

> 2 × 6 oz (150g) gammon steaks
> 1 tablespoon (15ml) soft brown sugar
> 1 tablespoon (15ml) wholegrain mustard
> 1 tablespoon (15ml) cider or orange juice

Pre-heat grill. Cook gammon steaks under a medium heat on one side for 4 minutes. Mix other ingredients together, turn gammon over and coat with the glaze. Cook for a further 3–4 minutes until glaze is bubbling and brown. Serve with new potatoes and a green salad or vegetables.

Tuna Stir-fry
Serves 2

8-oz (200-g) can tuna, drained
4 spring onions, chopped
8-oz (200-g) can baby sweetcorn or bamboo shoots
1 small red pepper, deseeded and thinly sliced
2 oz (50g) cashew nuts
1 tablespoon (15ml) oil
1 tablespoon (15ml) soy sauce
1 tablespoon (15ml) orange juice
1 tablespoon (15ml) tomato purée
1 tablespoon (15ml) wine or cider vinegar
1 teaspoon (5 ml) cornflour

Fry first five ingredients in oil until heated through. Mix other ingredients and add to pan, continue to cook for a minute or two until sauce thickens. Serve with rice.

Thai Okra and Peanut Curry
Serves 2

1 onion, chopped
1 clove garlic, chopped or crushed
1 tablespoon (15ml) oil
2 oz (50g) creamed coconut
1 tablespoon (15ml) Thai 7-spice seasoning
2 oz (50g) peanuts
8 oz (200g) okra, chopped
10 fl oz (250ml) orange juice

Fry onion and garlic in oil until browning. Make up the creamed coconut to a thick paste with hot water. Blend or purée the coconut, Thai seasoning and peanuts. Add with other ingredients to the pan and cook over a gentle heat until the okra is cooked through (about 20 minutes). Serve with rice or naan bread.

Salmon with Nutty Yoghurt Sauce
Serves 2

OK, it's not often that you can afford salmon when you're trying to stick to a budget. However, for the time when the fishmonger is selling it off cheaply at the end of the day, this is a lovely way of cooking it.

    2 × 4 oz (100g) salmon steaks or fillets
    1 tablespoon (15ml) oil
    5 fl oz (125ml) Greek yoghurt
    2 oz (50g) mixed chopped nuts
    sprinkling of chopped chives

Fry the salmon gently in the oil for 3–4 minutes on each side. Mix the yoghurt and nuts together. When salmon is cooked, serve with the sauce poured over the fish and sprinkled with chopped chives. This dish goes extremely well with new potatoes and fine green beans.

Grilled Garlic and Lime Chicken
Serves 2

    2 part-boned chicken breasts
    1 tablespoon (15ml) oil
    1 tablespoon (15ml) soy sauce
    grated rind and 1 tablespoon (15ml) juice of lime

Mix all ingredients together and, if possible, leave to marinate. (This would happily sit in the fridge all day if you had time to prepare it before leaving for work.) Pre-heat the grill, cook the chicken under a medium heat for 25 minutes, turning frequently and basting with the marinade mixture. Serve with new potatoes or rice salad and a green salad or vegetables.

Salmon and Broccoli Crunch
Serves 2

> 10 fl oz (250ml) white sauce (see p 9)
> sprinkling of mixed herbs
> 8-oz (200-g) can salmon, drained
> 4 oz (100g) broccoli florets
> 1 packet plain crisps

Pre-heat oven to 200°C/400°F/Gas 6. Mix the white sauce and herbs together. Put the salmon and broccoli in a ovenproof dish. Cover with the sauce. Sprinkle the crisps over the top so they cover dish. Cook in oven for 25 minutes. Serve with a green salad.

Mackerel with Orange Butter
Serves 2

> 2 mackerel, cleaned
> grated rind and juice of half an orange
> 1 oz (25g) butter, softened

Make three or four gashes in the side of each fish. Roll fish in orange juice. Beat together the butter and 1 tablespoon (15ml) orange juice. Spread half of orange butter over fish. Cook fish under a pre-heated medium grill for about 8 minutes on each side. Roll rest of butter into a log shape and put in fridge to harden. When fish is cooked, serve with slices of the orange butter on top. This goes well with new potatoes and a green salad or vegetable.

Tarragon Tart
Serves 4

>12 oz (300g) shortcrust pastry (see p 12)
>3 eggs, beaten
>5 fl oz (125ml) single cream
>2 tablespoons (30ml) fresh tarragon, chopped
>salt and pepper

Pre-heat oven to 200°C/400°F/Gas 6. Use the pastry to line an 8 in (20cm) flan tin. Prick the pastry base all over with a fork. Put some greaseproof paper on the base and weigh down with some coins. Cook in oven for 15 minutes. Beat the other ingredients together and pour into the pastry case (remove the paper and coins first!), then bake at 190°C/375°F/Gas 5 for 20–25 minutes until the filling has set. This tart is lovely served hot with new potatoes and vegetables or cold with salad.

Chillied Bean and Sausage Supper
Serves 2

>8-oz (200-g) can baked beans
>8-oz (200-g) can kidney beans, drained
>1 tablespoon (15ml) tomato purée
>2 teaspoons (10ml) chilli sauce
>4 oz (100g) salami stick, chopped
>1 tablespoon (15ml) soft margarine
>2 oz (50g) cheese, grated
>1 teaspoon (5ml) Worcester sauce
>4 slices of French bread

Put first five ingredients in a pan and warm through. Mix the margarine, cheese and Worcester sauce together. Put the bean and sausage mixture in an ovenproof dish, top with the bread and then spread the cheese mixture on top. Grill under a pre-heated medium grill for a few minutes until cheese is bubbling and turning brown. Serve immediately.

Cheesy Pasta Bake
Serves 2

10 fl oz (250ml) cheese sauce (see p 9)
2 oz (50g) sweetcorn
2 oz (50g) peas, cooked
6 oz (150g) pasta shapes, cooked
salt and pepper
1 packet cheese and onion crisps
1 oz (50g) cheese, grated

Mix the cheese sauce, sweetcorn, peas and pasta and season well. Put into an ovenproof dish and then cover with the crisps and cheese. Cook under a pre-heated medium grill until cheese is bubbling and topping is browning. Serve immediately with a crunchy salad.

Pork and Prawn Frittata
Serves 2

1 tablespoon (15ml) oil
4 spring onions, chopped
4 oz (100g) white cabbage, finely shredded
1 teaspoon (5ml) ginger purée
1 teaspoon (5ml) soy sauce
4 oz (100g) prawns
4 oz (100g) pork, cooked and chopped
4 eggs, beaten

Put all ingredients except eggs in a frying pan and cook quickly until cabbage is slightly soft. Add eggs and stir once. Leave to cook on a medium heat for 3 minutes or until eggs have nearly set. Put under a grill to cook the top of the frittata. Serve with salad.

Tuna and Pepper Quiche
Serves 2

    12 oz (300g) cheese pastry (see p 12)
    1 red pepper, deseeded and chopped
    1 green pepper, deseeded and chopped
    2 tablespoons (30ml) soft margarine or butter
    8-oz (200-g) can tuna, drained
    2 eggs, beaten
    3 fl oz (75ml) double cream
    salt and pepper
    sprinkling of Tabasco sauce

Pre-heat oven to 200°C/400°F/Gas 6. Line an 8 in (20 cm) flan tin with the pastry. Prick holes all over the base, weigh down with greaseproof paper and coins. Cook in pre-heated oven for 15 minutes. Meanwhile, fry peppers in margarine or butter. Remove paper and coins from pastry and put tuna and peppers into flan case. Beat other ingredients together and pour into flan. Bake at 190°C/375°F/Gas 5 for 20 minutes.

Cheese and Bacon Turnovers
Serves 2

    8 oz (200g) bought flaky pastry
    6 oz (150g) cooked potato, cubed
    4 oz (100g) streaky bacon, cooked and chopped
    2 oz (50g) cheese, grated
    10 fl oz (250ml) cheese sauce (see p 9)
    black pepper
    pinch of sage
    milk to glaze

Pre-heat oven to 220°C/425°F/Gas 7. Divide pastry into 2 balls, roll each into an 8 in (20cm) circle. Bind together the potato, bacon and cheese with 1–2 tablespoons (15–30ml) of the cheese sauce and season with pepper and sage. Divide mixture between circles, turn one side of circle over filling and seal edges together, crimping edges together. Brush with milk and cook on a baking tray for 25–30 minutes until pastry is cooked and risen. Serve with remaining sauce (heated through) and a green vegetable.

Chicken Breasts with Cream Tarragon Sauce
Serves 2

2 chicken breasts, skinned and boned
1 tablespoon (15ml) flour
1 tablespoon (15ml) paprika
2 tablespoons (30ml) soft margarine or butter
sprinkling of tarragon
5 fl oz (125ml) double cream
black pepper

Mix together the chicken, flour and paprika. Shake off excess flour and fry chicken in margarine or butter until brown on all sides. Add tarragon and cream and season with pepper. Cover pan tightly and cook gently for about 15–20 minutes until chicken is cooked through. Serve with new potatoes and green beans or broccoli.

Mexican Chicken
Serves 2

12 oz (300g) chicken, skinned
1 pepper, deseeded and chopped
1 onion, chopped
2 tablespoons (30ml) olive oil
8-oz (200-g) can sweetcorn, drained
sprinkling of paprika
1 teaspoon (5ml) garlic purée
8-oz (200-g) can chopped tomatoes
few chopped olives
1 tablespoon (15ml) cream

Pre-heat oven to 190°C/375°F/Gas 5. Fry chicken, pepper and onion in oil for 10 minutes. Add sweetcorn, paprika and garlic purée and cook for another 5 minutes. Add all other ingredients except cream and transfer to an ovenproof dish. Cook in pre-heated oven for 25 minutes. Stir in cream before serving with rice or garlic bread.

Salmon Cream Sauce and Pasta
Serves 2

> 6 oz (150g) pasta
> 1 small onion, finely chopped
> 1 tablespoon (15ml) olive oil
> 8-oz (200-g) can pink salmon, drained
> sprinkling of paprika
> 5 fl oz (125ml) double cream
> 2 teaspoons (10ml) tomato purée
> black pepper

Cook pasta as directed on packet. Fry onion in oil until soft, stir in all other ingredients until blended together. When pasta is cooked, drain and serve with sauce.

Aubergine and Tomato Bake
Serves 2

> 1 onion, chopped
> 2 cloves garlic, crushed
> olive oil
> 1 aubergine, cut lengthways and sliced
> 14-oz (400-g) can chopped tomatoes
> 2 tablespoons (30ml) tomato purée
> salt and pepper
> 2 tablespoons (30ml) fresh parsley, chopped

Pre-heat oven to 180°C/350°F/Gas 4. Fry the onion and garlic in some oil until soft, and transfer to an ovenproof dish. Fry the aubergine slices, a few at a time – you will need quite a lot of oil for this. As they are done, put in ovenproof dish. Finally, add all other ingredients and 2 tablespoons (30ml) olive oil. Cook in pre-heated oven for 40 minutes. Leave until luke-warm and serve with garlic bread. This dish can also be eaten cold as a salad.

Chicken in Parmesan Cream
Serves 2

    1 tablespoon (15ml) breadcrumbs
    2 tablespoons (30ml) Parmesan cheese
    2 chicken breasts, skinned and boned
    1 tablespoon (15ml) soft margarine or butter
    2 tablespoons (30ml) cream
    10 fl oz (250ml) cheese sauce made with Parmesan
      cheese (see p 9)

Pre-heat oven to 180°C/350°F/Gas 4. Mix the breadcrumbs
with half the Parmesan cheese. Coat the chicken with breadcrumb mix and fry in margarine or butter until brown on all
sides. Add cream to cheese sauce and put half of sauce in
ovenproof dish. Transfer chicken to dish and cover with
remaining sauce. Sprinkle with rest of Parmesan. Bake in
pre-heated oven for 30 minutes until brown. Serve with new
potatoes and broccoli.

Chicken and Broccoli Turnovers
Serves 2

    8 oz (200g) flaky pastry
    8 oz (200g) cooked chicken, shredded
    4 oz (100g) cooked broccoli florets
    10 fl oz (250ml) cheese sauce (see p 9)
    dash of Tabasco sauce
    salt and pepper
    milk to glaze

Pre-heat oven to 220°C/425°F/Gas 7. Divide pastry into 2
balls, roll each out into an 8 in (20cm) circle. Bind together
the chicken and broccoli with a little of the cheese sauce and
season with Tabasco and salt and pepper. Divide mixture
between circles and turn one edge over filling to seal edges
and crimp together. Brush with milk and cook on a baking
tray in pre-heated oven for 25–30 minutes until pastry is
cooked and risen. Serve with remaining sauce (heated
through) and carrots.

Sole Meunière
Serves 2

> 2 sole fillets
> 1 tablespoon (15ml) flour
> 1 tablespoon (15ml) paprika
> 2 tablespoons (30ml) butter
> lemon juice
> black pepper
> sprinkling of chopped parsley

Coat the fish in the flour and paprika. Heat the butter and gently fry the fish until brown on both sides (3–4 minutes each side). Serve fish with butter poured over and sprinkled with lemon juice, pepper and parsley. Best with new potatoes and peas.

Sweet 'n' Sour Prawns
Serves 2

> 1 red pepper, deseeded and chopped
> 1 teaspoon (5ml) garlic purée
> 1 teaspoon (5ml) ginger purée
> 1 tablespoon (15ml) oil
> 1 tablespoon (15ml) tomato ketchup
> 1 tablespoon (15ml) vinegar
> 1 tablespoon (15ml) brown sugar
> 2 tablespoons (30ml) soy sauce
> 8 oz (200g) prawns

Fry pepper, garlic and ginger in oil for 3 minutes, add rest of ingredients and stir-fry for 2 minutes. Serve with rice.

Chicken Korma
Serves 2

1 onion, chopped
1 teaspoon (5ml) garlic purée
1 teaspoon (5ml) ginger purée
1 tablespoon (15 ml) oil
12 oz (300g) chicken breast, skinned and boned
1 tablespoon (15ml) soft margarine or butter
1 tablespoon (15ml) mild curry paste
8 fl oz (200ml) Greek yoghurt
1 tablespoon (15ml) ground almonds
1 tablespoon (15ml) lemon juice

Fry the onion, garlic and ginger in oil until soft. Cut chicken into bite-sized pieces, add to pan with curry paste and margarine or butter, continue to cook for 10 minutes until chicken is brown. Add other ingredients and stir well. Cover tightly and simmer very gently for 15 minutes. Serve with shelled pistachio nuts, chopped finely, and rice and poppadoms.

Cheese Croquettes
Serves 2

8 oz (200g) cooked rice
2 oz (50g) cheese, grated
2 oz (50g) chopped mixed nuts
1 teaspoon (5ml) tomato purée
sprinkling of Tabasco sauce
1 egg, beaten
dried breadcrumbs
oil, for frying

Mix all ingredients except breadcrumbs and oil. Shape into little rolls. Coat in breadcrumbs and fry in oil until golden brown. Serve with tomato ketchup or chutney and a salad.

Chicken and Corn-stuffed Jackets
Serves 2

> 2 × 6–8 oz (2 × 150–200g) baking potatoes
> oil
> 4 oz (100g) cooked chicken, shredded
> 4 oz (100g) sweetcorn
> 1 tablespoon (15ml) soft margarine or butter
> 1 tablespoon (15ml) mayonnaise
> salt and pepper

Pre-heat oven to 200°C/400°F/Gas 6. Brush potatoes with oil. Bake in pre-heated oven for 75 minutes. Scoop out potato flesh and mash with other ingredients, pile back into jackets and brown under a hot grill. Serve with salad and garlic bread.

Stuffed Courgettes
Serves 2

> 4 courgettes
> 2 tomatoes, chopped
> 2 teaspoons (10ml) tomato purée
> 1 tablespoon (15ml) olive oil
> 2 tablespoons (30ml) hazelnuts, chopped
> sprinkling of Italian seasoning
> sprinkling of Tabasco sauce

Pre-heat oven to 190°C/375°F/Gas 5. Cut one side off each courgette and, on opposite side, cut a sliver of skin so that courgette sits flatly on the plate. Next scoop out inside flesh (leaving ends and a thickish shell – so you have a mini boat), finely chop flesh and fry with tomato in oil until soft. Mix in the other ingredients and use this mixture to stuff courgettes. Place courgettes on a baking tray and cook in pre-heated oven for 25 minutes. Serve with chips or new potatoes and peas.

Chicken with Tomato Butter
Serves 2

>   1 tablespoon (15ml) tomato ketchup
>   2 oz (50g) butter, softened
>   salt and pepper
>   2 chicken breasts, skinned and boned

Mix tomato ketchup, butter and seasoning together. Rub a little of mixture onto chicken. Shape the rest into 2 pats and refrigerate. Cook chicken under a medium grill, turning frequently for 15–20 minutes, until cooked and brown. Serve with tomato butter. Good with baked or new potatoes and a green vegetable.

Cheese Omelette
Serves 1

For those times when for one reason or another you are eating alone, this is the perfect answer. You can vary the filling, putting in whatever you have in the fridge. I just happen to prefer a simple cheese omelette. A perfect omelette will be golden underneath and still a little creamy on top.

>   2–3 eggs (depending on appetite)
>   1 tablespoon (15ml) cold water
>   salt and pepper
>   2 oz (50g) cheese, grated
>   knob of butter
>   sprinkling of Tabasco sauce (optional)

Beat the eggs and then add water and season to taste. To this mixture add half the grated cheese. Heat a frying or omelette pan. When hot add the butter and swirl around, letting it melt. Quickly add the egg mixture and, with a wooden spoon, keep drawing the egg into the middle letting the uncooked egg run to the sides of the pan. When the egg has set, leave to cook for 1 minute. Mix the Tabasco and remaining cheese, place filling in middle of omelette and slide on to a plate, folding one side over the other as you do so (some people prefer to fold both sides on top of each other and then tip omelette out with folds underneath – do whatever you think is easiest). Serve with peas and sweetcorn.

Baconburgers
Serves 2

    4 oz (100g) back bacon, fat removed
    half a small onion
    salt and pepper
    pinch of sage
    beaten egg
    oil, for frying

Mince the bacon and onion. Season with salt, pepper and sage, bind together using a little egg. On a floured surface shape into 4 balls and flatten into beefburger shapes. Fry gently in oil for 6–8 minutes, turning to ensure even cooking, until golden brown. Serve with chips or new potatoes and baked beans or tomato salad.

Pork Chops with Pineapple
Serves 2

    2 pork chops
    8-oz (200-g) can pineapple rings in natural juice
    sprinkling of brown sugar
    sprinkling of Tabasco sauce

Pre-heat oven to 190°C/375°F/Gas 5. Place pork chops in an ovenproof dish and then pour in juice from tinned pineapple. Cover and cook in pre-heated oven for 40 minutes. Pour off remaining juice and place pineapple rings on top of meat, sprinkle with sugar and Tabasco sauce. Return to oven for 5–10 minutes until sugar has melted. Serve with mashed potato and cabbage.

Chicken Hash
Serves 2

> 1 onion, chopped
> 1 tablespoon (15ml) soft margarine or butter
> 12 oz (300g) cooked chicken, shredded
> 10 fl oz (250ml) cheese sauce (see p 9)
> salt and pepper
> 1 egg yolk, beaten
> 2 oz (50g) cheese, grated

Pre-heat oven to 200°C/400°F/Gas 6. Fry onion in margarine or butter until soft. Mix chicken, onion and half of cheese sauce together. Season. Place in an ovenproof dish, beat egg yolk into rest of cheese sauce and stir in half the cheese. Spoon over chicken mixture, spreading evenly, sprinkle with remaining cheese. Bake in pre-heated oven for 25 minutes until top is brown. Serve with broccoli and a tomato salad.

Chicken Provençale
Serves 2

> 1 onion, chopped
> 1 clove garlic, chopped
> 1 green pepper, deseeded and chopped
> 2 tablespoons (30ml) olive oil
> 12 oz (300g) chicken meat, skinned
> 14-oz (400-g) can chopped tomatoes
> 1 tablespoon (15ml) tomato purée
> sprinkling of herbes de Provence
> glass of dry white wine or chicken stock
> sprinkling of chopped olives
> sprinkling of parsley

Pre-heat oven to 180°C/350°F/Gas 4. Fry onion, garlic and pepper in oil until soft, add chicken and cook until brown, place in ovenproof dish with rest of ingredients. Cover tightly and cook in pre-heated oven for 45–60 minutes until chicken is cooked (when prodded with a skewer or sharp knife the juices run clear). Serve with rice and peas or carrots.

Chicken in Mustard Cream
Serves 2

12 oz (300g) chicken breasts, skinned and boned
2 tablespoons (30ml) soft margarine or butter.
1 tablespoon (15ml) French mustard
5 fl oz (125ml) single cream
black pepper

Pre-heat oven to 180°C/350°F/Gas 4. Cut chicken into bite-sized pieces. Fry in margarine or butter until brown on all sides. Stir in mustard and then cream. Place in an ovenproof dish, cover tightly. Cook in pre-heated oven for 30 minutes. Serve with jacket potatoes and broccoli.

Stuffed Aubergine
Serves 2

1 large aubergine, halved
1 onion, chopped
1 clove garlic, crushed
2 tablespoons (30ml) olive oil
2 oz (50g) mushrooms, chopped
8-oz (200-g) can chopped tomatoes
1 tablespoon (15ml) tomato purée
sprinkling of Italian herbs
1 tablespoon (15ml) fresh parsley, chopped
2 tablespoons (30ml) fresh breadcrumbs
1 tablespoon (15ml) chopped mixed nuts

Pre-heat oven to 200°C/400°F/Gas 6. Scoop out the aubergine flesh, leaving two shells. Place shells in shallow ovenproof dish. Chop flesh and fry gently with onion and garlic in oil for 10 minutes. Add mushrooms and fry for a further minute before mixing in tomatoes, tomato purée and herbs. Use this mixture to stuff shells. Dry-fry breadcrumbs and nuts for a few minutes until brown and then sprinkle over aubergine. Bake in pre-heated oven for 25 minutes. Serve with garlic bread and salad.

3 Summer

At last those long hot summer days have arrived . . . This is the season of strawberries and cream, of barbecues and picnics, when the evening stretches invitingly ahead of you and no one in their right mind is going to spend hours in front of a hot stove. So the essence of summer cooking is in using fresh ingredients which only need the briefest of cooking time – if any!

Fruit and vegetables are available in abundance and are also extremely cheap. In the summer I find that nine times out of ten when I am cooking it is in one of two ways, either with the grill or my trusty wok. I also use a lot of pickles and bottled sauces at this time; there are always new ones on the market so keep a lookout for new flavours to jazz up simple grilled meats.

Vegetable Stir-fry
Serves 2

 1 tablespoon (15ml) oil
 1 red pepper, deseeded and cut into strips
 1 green pepper, deseeded and cut into strips
 1 courgette, cut into rounds
 4 oz (100g) mushrooms, sliced
 1 teaspoon (5ml) garlic purée
 1 teaspoon (5ml) ginger purée
 1 tablespoon (15ml) soy sauce
 2 tablespoons (30ml) sherry or orange juice

Heat the oil in a wok or large frying pan. Add all the
vegetables with the garlic and ginger purées and quickly
stir-fry for 2 minutes. Add the soy sauce and sherry or orange
and fry for a further minute. Serve immediately with rice or
noodles.

Egg and Bacon Salad
Serves 2

This dish originated when we had friends staying; we had all had a little too much to drink the night before and consequently were very late getting up the next morning. Nobody fancied going to the pub for lunch and all I had in the house were the ingredients for our missed breakfast. I picked some spinach leaves from the garden (just about the only vegetable we grow!) and concocted this salad – it's delicious and makes an excellent brunch dish. So my thanks to Sarah – if she hadn't made up that last jug of Pimms, this dish would never have been invented.

     2 hard boiled eggs, quartered
     4 bacon rashers, grilled and chopped
     8 oz (200g) fresh spinach leaves, washed
     2 oz (50g) mushrooms, sliced
     2 tomatoes, sliced
     2 tablespoons (30ml) mustard salad dressing
     sprinkling of salad croûtons (or fried onion bits)

Arrange the egg, bacon and vegetables in your salad bowls or plates, drizzle with the dressing and then sprinkle with the croûtons (or fried onion bits). Serve immediately. Garlic bread goes very well with this salad.

Fish with Lemon Sauce
Serves 2

> 2 white fish fillets
> 5 fl oz (125ml) hot fish stock
> 5 fl oz (125ml) hot milk
> 1 lemon, sliced
> 5 fl oz (125ml) natural yoghurt
> 1 tablespoon (15ml) cornflour
> knob of butter

Put the fish fillets in the bottom of a saucepan and cover with the stock and milk. Remove any seeds from the lemon, reserve 2 slices and put the rest in the saucepan. Simmer gently for 6 minutes until fish is white and firm. Remove the fish carefully and keep warm (cover with foil and put in a cool oven). Discard the lemon from the sauce, squeezing as much juice as possible from the slices as you remove them. Blend the yoghurt and cornflour and then whisk into the sauce. Bring to the boil and then simmer for 2 minutes, stirring. When the sauce has thickened, add the butter and, when it has melted, serve the fish covered with the sauce, garnished with the reserved lemon slices. This is lovely served with minted new potatoes and peas or courgettes.

Ham and Courgette Gratin
Serves 2

> 10 fl oz (250ml) white sauce (see p 9)
> 8 oz (200g) courgettes, grated
> 4 oz (100g) ham, diced
> salt and pepper
> 2 oz (50g) cheese, grated
> 3 eggs

Pre-heat oven to 190°C/375°F/Gas 5. Mix the white sauce with the courgettes and ham and season well. Add half the cheese and stir well. Remove from the heat. Separate the eggs and whisk the whites. Beat the yolks, add them to the courgette mixture and mix well. Gently mix in the whisked whites. Put into a greased ovenproof dish and sprinkle with the remaining cheese. Cook in the pre-heated oven for 25–30 minutes until the mixture has risen and is golden brown. This can be served hot or cold with salad.

Pan-fried Fish Steaks
Serves 2

> 2 tablespoons (30ml) oil
> knob of butter
> 2 thin leeks, sliced
> 2 × 6 oz (2 × 150g) fish steaks
> 2 tablespoons (30ml) apple juice

Heat 1 tablespoon (15ml) of the oil with the butter, add the leeks and cook for a few minutes until soft, remove from the pan. Add the rest of the oil and then the fish steaks, fry for approximately 3–4 minutes on each side until brown. Return the leeks to the pan and sprinkle with the apple juice. Cover and cook for a further 2 minutes. Serve with new potatoes and sweetcorn.

Crispy Cheesy Fish
Serves 2

    2 × 6 oz (2 × 150g) mullet fillets
    1 teaspoon (5ml) chilli sauce or paste
    3 tablespoons (45ml) double cream
    2 oz (50g) cheese, finely grated
    2 tablespoons (30ml) dried breadcrumbs
    1 tablespoon (15ml) parsley, roughly chopped

Pre-heat oven to 180°F/350°C/Gas 4. Place the fillets in an oiled ovenproof dish. Drizzle with the chilli sauce, then cover with the cream. Mix the cheese, breadcrumbs and parsley together and sprinkle over the fish. Cook in the pre-heated oven for 20 minutes until crispy and brown. Serve with new potatoes and a watercress salad.

Hot Potato and Salami Salad
Serves 2

    2 tablespoons (30ml) olive oil
    1 small onion, sliced
    2 cloves garlic, crushed or chopped
    1 red pepper, deseeded and sliced
    4 oz (100g) salami, unsliced
    8 oz (200g) baby new potatoes, cooked
    1 tablespoon (15ml) red wine or sherry vinegar
    sprinkling of chives
    sprinkling of pitted black olives

Heat 1 tablespoon (15ml) of the oil and gently fry the onion, garlic and pepper. Dice the salami, add to the pan with the potato and heat through. Remove from the heat and add the remaining oil and vinegar, stir well. Arrange on plates and sprinkle with the chives and olives. Serve immediately.

Bacon and Rice Stir-fry
Serves 2

> 8 oz (200g) mushrooms, sliced
> 4 oz (100g) bacon, chopped
> 2 tablespoons (30ml) oil
> 1 tablespoon (15ml) sherry vinegar
> 4 oz (100g) brown rice, cooked
> sprinkling of Parmesan cheese
> sprinkling of parsley

Fry the mushrooms and bacon in oil until bacon is cooked through. Add the vinegar and rice and heat through. Serve immediately sprinkled with Parmesan cheese and parsley. This is wonderful with a tomato side salad.

Mediterranean Casserole
Serves 4

> 3 peppers of mixed colours, deseeded and cut into
>   chunks
> 8 cloves garlic, unskinned
> 1 large onion, sliced
> 4 tablespoons (60ml) olive oil
> 2 chicken breasts, 2 wings and 2 legs
> 14-oz (400-g) can chopped tomatoes
> pinch of sugar
> 2 tablespoons (30ml) parsley, chopped
> salt and pepper
> sprinkling of pitted black olives
> fresh basil leaves, to garnish

Pre-heat oven to 180°C/350°F/Gas 4. Gently fry peppers, garlic and onion in oil until soft, remove to an ovenproof dish. Cut each chicken breast into two and then fry all chicken pieces until brown. Place in ovenproof dish with tomatoes, sugar, parsley and seasoning. Cover and cook in a pre-heated oven for 1 hour until chicken is cooked through. Serve sprinkled with the olives and garnished with the basil. This can be eaten hot or cold and can be served with new potatoes or rice salad. It is particularly good with a salad made from thinly sliced red onions and mushrooms or spinach leaves dressed with lemon and tahini.

Sardine Bake
Serves 2

> 1 lemon, sliced
> 4 sardines, cleaned, scaled and heads removed
> 6 firm tomatoes, sliced
> 1 tablespoon (15ml) fresh basil, chopped
> 1 tablespoon (15ml) fresh parsley, chopped
> 1 clove garlic, chopped
> 2 tablespoons (30ml) olive oil
> salt and pepper

Pre-heat oven to 180°C/350°/Gas 4. Place half a lemon slice in each sardine. Put a layer of lemon and tomatoes in the bottom of a greased ovenproof dish. Place sardines on this layer and then cover with the rest of lemon and tomatoes. Sprinkle with herbs, garlic and oil, season well. Cook in pre-heated oven for 20 minutes until the fish is cooked and browning on top. Serve with garlic bread and a watercress or spinach salad.

Bacon-wrapped Trout
Serves 2

> 2 rainbow trout, cleaned and scaled (and boned if possible)
> 4 rashers streaky bacon
> 1 lemon
> parsley, to garnish

Pre-heat oven to 180°C/350°F/Gas 4. Wrap each trout in two rashers of bacon. Quarter the lemon and reserve two quarters for garnish. Put trout in a greased ovenproof dish, squeeze lemon over trout and cook in a pre-heated oven for 15–20 minutes until fish is cooked and bacon is crisping. (Alternatively grill under a hot grill for 8 minutes, turning once, but this is trickier.) Garnish with parsley and serve with new potatoes and broccoli.

Spicy Piperade
Serves 2

   2 tablespoons (30ml) olive oil
   1 onion, sliced
   2 cloves garlic, chopped or crushed
   1 red pepper, deseeded and sliced
   7-oz (200-g) can chopped tomatoes
   1 teaspoon (5ml) chilli sauce or paste
   1 teaspoon (5ml) pesto
   2 teaspoons (10ml) tomato purée
   3 eggs, beaten

Heat the oil and gently fry the onion, garlic and pepper until soft. Add all other ingredients except eggs and leave to simmer gently for 5 minutes until sauce has reduced and thickened. Add eggs and, stirring continuously, continue to cook until eggs are creamy and barely set. Serve immediately with garlic bread.

Ham and Pasta Bake
Serves 4

   1 lb (400g) leeks, sliced
   1 tablespoon (5ml) oil
   4 eggs, beaten
   2 fl oz (50ml) single cream
   dash of Tabasco sauce
   8 oz (200g) ham, diced
   4 oz (100g) cheese, grated
   4 oz (100g) macaroni, cooked
   sprinkling of cayenne pepper

Pre-heat oven to 180°C/350°F/Gas 4. Put the leeks and oil in a covered saucepan and cook over a gentle heat for 10 minutes. Whisk the eggs and cream together and season with Tabasco. Add the ham, cheese and macaroni, mix well. Put into a well greased ovenproof dish, sprinkle with cayenne pepper and cook in pre-heated oven for 25–30 minutes until the top is golden brown. Serve hot or cold with salad.

Gingery Coconut Chicken Kebabs
Serves 2

2 teaspoons (10ml) ginger purée
2 tablespoons (30ml) dessicated coconut
2 teaspoons (10ml) brown sugar
juice of 1 lime
1 tablespoon (15ml) oil
2 chicken breasts, skinned, boned and cubed

Mix all ingredients together and leave to marinate in the fridge for 4–24 hours. Put chicken on to skewers or satay sticks and grill under a hot grill for 6 minutes, until cooked and brown. Serve with rice and a sauce made from Greek yogurt mixed with a little garlic and lemon juice or tahini. This is also nice with **Banana Chutney** – dice a banana very finely and add 1 teaspoon (5ml) sherry vinegar and a dash of Tabasco sauce.

Greek Lamb Kebabs
Serves 2

2 lean lamb steaks, cubed
1 green pepper, deseeded and cubed
1 tablespoon (15ml) olive oil
1 tablespoon (15ml) white wine
squeeze of lemon juice
2 cloves garlic, crushed
sprinkling of dried thyme

Mix all ingredients and marinate in the fridge for 4–24 hours. Thread lamb and pepper on to skewers or satay sticks and brush with marinade. Cook under a hot grill for 8 minutes until meat is cooked and peppers are brown at edges. Serve with a rice and tomato salad.

Walnut, Stilton and Broccoli Flan
Serves 4

> 12 oz (300g) shortcrust pastry (see p 12)
> 6 oz (150g) broccoli florets, cooked
> 4 eggs, beaten
> 10 fl oz (250ml) milk
> 5 fl oz (125ml) single cream
> 2 teaspoons (10ml) cornflour
> black pepper
> 4 oz (100g) Stilton, crumbled
> 1 oz (25g) walnuts, chopped

Pre-heat oven to 200°C/400°F/Gas 6. Roll out the pastry and line an 8 in (20 cm) flan dish. Use a fork to prick holes in the bottom of the base. Put a layer of greaseproof paper on the base and weigh down with coins, bake in pre-heated oven for 20 minutes until pastry is cooked.

Remove coins and greaseproof paper. Put broccoli into the flan, mix eggs, milk, cream and cornflour together, season with pepper, and pour over broccoli. Sprinkle Stilton into flan. Cook at same heat for 15 minutes, then sprinkle with walnuts and cook for a further 10 minutes. Serve hot or cold with salad.

Grilled Thai Chicken
Serves 2

> 2 chicken breasts, skinned
> 1 tablespoon (15ml) oil
> 1 teaspoon (5ml) Thai-7-spice
> ½ teaspoon (2.5ml) dried lemon grass
> 1 teaspoon (5ml) ginger purée
> 1 teaspoon (5ml) soy sauce
> 2 teaspoons (10ml) fresh lime juice

Put all ingredients into a bowl, cover and marinate in the fridge for 4–24 hours. Turn occasionally. Grill under a pre-heated medium grill for 25 minutes, turning frequently, until the chicken is cooked. Serve hot or cold with rice and salad.

Fried Mustardy Herring
Serves 2

1 tablespoon (15ml) double cream
1 egg yolk
1 tablespoon (15ml) French mustard
2 × 4 oz (2 × 100g) herrings, cleaned and heads
  removed
2 tablespoons (30ml) pinhead oatmeal
1 tablespoon (15ml) oil
knob of butter
parsley, to garnish

Mix the cream, egg yolk and mustard together and use to coat the outsides of the herring. Cover and marinate for 4–24 hours in a fridge. Heat the oil and butter and gently fry the herring on both sides until brown and cooked (approximately 8 minutes). Serve garnished with the parsley, with new potatoes and peas or a tomato salad.

Veggie Burgers
Serves 2

3 oz (75g) fresh wholemeal breadcrumbs
2 oz (50g) mushrooms, finely chopped
1 small onion, finely chopped
2 oz (50g) ground nuts
1 egg, beaten
salt and pepper

Combine all ingredients, mixing well. Leave to stand for 30 minutes. Divide mixture into four. Take each portion in turn and shape into a burger (try not to handle too much). Grill or fry gently for 4 minutes on each side. Serve with new potatoes or chips and salad.

Prawn and Nut Stir-fry
Serves 2

- 1 tablespoon (15ml) oil
- 4 oz (100g) cashew nuts
- 2 sticks celery, sliced
- 1 red pepper, deseeded and sliced
- 2 cloves garlic, crushed or chopped
- 8 oz (200g) shelled prawns
- 1 tablespoon (15ml) cornflour
- 1 tablespoon (15ml) soy sauce

Heat the oil in a wok or large frying pan. Stir-fry the nuts, celery, pepper and garlic for 2 minutes. Mix the prawns with the cornflour. (A good way to do this is to put them in a plastic bag and shake together.) Add to the other stir-fry ingredients. Stir-fry prawn and nut mixture for 1 minute before adding soy sauce and cooking for a further minute. Serve with rice.

Lamb Piri-piri
Serves 2

- 2 leg of lamb steaks
- 1 tablespoon (15ml) oil
- 1 tablespoon (15ml) orange juice
- 2 teaspoons (10ml) piri-piri seasoning

Mix all ingredients together and leave to marinate in the fridge for 4–24 hours. Grill lamb under a medium heat for 10 minutes, turning once. Serve with new potatoes and spinach leaves dressed with yogurt and lemon juice.

Courgette and Nut Roast
Serves 4

8 oz (200g) mixed nuts, toasted and finely chopped
1 lb (400g) courgettes, grated
4 oz (100g) fresh wholemeal breadcrumbs
1 red pepper, deseeded and finely chopped
1 tablespoon (15ml) oil
1 onion, finely chopped
1 tablespoon (15ml) pesto
2 eggs, beaten

Pre-heat oven to 190°C/375°F/Gas 5. Mix all ingredients together and place in a well greased ovenproof dish. Cook in pre-heated oven for 40 minutes until firm to the touch and brown on top. Remove from oven and leave to rest for 5 minutes. Cut into squares and serve hot or cold. This is particularly good with tomato sauce, new potatoes and a green vegetable or salad.

Indonesian Chicken Salad
Serves 2

5 fl oz (125ml) natural yoghurt
2 tablespoons (30ml) mango chutney
1 tablespoon (15ml) mild curry paste
1 oz (25g) sultanas
1 tablespoon (15ml) double cream
12 oz (300g) cooked chicken meat, cubed
12 oz (300g) cooked potatoes, cubed

Combine the yoghurt, mango chutney, curry paste, sultanas and cream, mix well. Stir in chicken and potatoes. Chill before serving. Serve with rice salad and a tomato and onion salad.

Greek Lamb
Serves 4

1.5 lb (600g) lean lamb, cubed
2 tablespoons (30ml) olive oil
1 lb (400g) shallots, peeled but left whole
16-oz (400-g) can chopped tomatoes
pinch of sugar
1 lemon, grated rind and 1 tablespoon (15ml) juice
3 whole cloves
10 fl oz (250ml) red wine
salt and pepper

Pre-heat oven to 180°C/350°F/Gas 4. Fry lamb in oil until brown on all sides. Add shallots and fry until starting to take colour. Add rest of ingredients, seasoning well. Transfer to a ovenproof dish. Cook in pre-heated oven for 1 hour 15 minutes. Remove and let cool slightly before serving. This is good with garlic bread and salad or, if left to cool completely, with rice salad and mushrooms à la grecque.

Grilled Chinese Chops
Serves 2

2 pork loin chops
rind and juice of 1 orange
1 tablespoon (15ml) sweet chilli sauce
1 tablespoon (15ml) runny honey
1 teaspoon (5ml) ginger purée
1 teaspoon (5ml) garlic purée
sprinkling of Chinese 5-spice powder

Combine all ingredients and leave to marinate for 4–24 hours, covered, in the fridge. Grill chops under a medium heat for 5 minutes on each side. Serve with new potatoes and a green vegetable.

Fruity Lamb Pilau
Serves 4

> 1 onion, sliced
> 1 tablespoon (15ml) oil
> 6 oz (150g) brown rice
> 15 fl oz (375ml) hot lamb stock
> 1 lb (400g) cooked lamb, cubed
> 4 oz (100g) no-need-to-soak apricots, quartered
> pinch of cinnamon
> parsley, to garnish

Fry onion in oil until soft. Add the rice and half the stock. Cook for 10 minutes, add the remaining stock and remaining ingredients (except parsley). Continue to cook until stock is absorbed. Garnish with parsley. Serve hot with a green vegetable or cold with salad.

Lamb in Orange Sauce
Serves 2

> 2 leg of lamb steaks
> knob of butter
> black pepper
> 2 teaspoons (10ml) cornflour
> 5 fl oz (125ml) orange juice
> sprinkling of coriander
> grated rind and segments of 1 orange

Spread the lamb with some butter and season with pepper. Grill under a medium heat for 5 minutes each side. Meanwhile, to make the sauce, blend the cornflour with a little of the juice whilst heating the rest of the juice gently. When simmering, add the cornflour mixture and stir until it thickens. Add the coriander, orange rind and segments. Heat through. Serve the steaks with the sauce poured over. This is very good with new potatoes and green beans.

Lamb and Pepper Stir-fry
Serves 2

    1 onion, chopped
    1 red pepper, deseeded and sliced
    1 green pepper, deseeded and sliced
    1 tablespoon (15ml) oil
    4 oz (100g) minced lamb
    3 tablespoons (45ml) hot lamb stock
    2 tablespoons (30ml) black bean sauce
    1 tablespoon (15ml) runny honey

Stir-fry the onion and peppers in the oil for 3 minutes. Add the lamb and continue to fry for a further 2 minutes. Add the stock, black bean sauce and honey. Cook for a further minute. Serve with rice.

Pork Paprika
Serves 2

    1 onion, chopped
    1 red pepper, deseeded and cut into diamond shapes
    1 tablespoon (15ml) oil
    knob of butter
    2 pork chops, fat removed and meat cubed
    1 tablespoon (15ml) paprika
    4 tablespoons (60ml) single cream

Fry onion and pepper in oil and butter until soft, then add pork and paprika, and cook for 5 minutes, stirring continuously. Add cream and heat through – do not boil. Serve with buttered noodles and broccoli.

Tikka Fish Fillets
Serves 2

> 1 tablespoon (15ml) tikka paste
> 1 tablespoon (15ml) oil
> 2 tablespoons (30ml) natural yoghurt
> 2 flat fish fillets

Mix tikka paste, oil and yoghurt together. Place fish fillets on a grill pan and cover with yoghurt mixture. Grill under a medium heat for 2–3 minutes each side. Serve with new potatoes and a watercress salad.

Lamb with Mint Mustard
Serves 2

> 2 lamb chops
> 2 teaspoons (10ml) mint sauce
> 2 teaspoons (10ml) wholegrain mustard

Cook the lamb chops under a medium grill for about 4 minutes on each side until cooked through and brown (any fat on chops should be cooked until starting to crisp). Mix the mint sauce and mustard together and serve with lamb chops. This is very good with new potatoes and runner beans.

Tuna-stuffed Jackets
Serves 2

> 2 × 6–8 oz (2 × 150–200g) baking potatoes
> oil
> 8-oz (200-g) can tuna, drained
> 2 tablespoons (30ml) mayonnaise
> 1 tablespoon (15ml) soft margarine or butter
> salt and pepper

Pre-heat oven to 200°C/400°F/Gas 6. Brush the potatoes with oil and cook in pre-heated oven for 75 minutes. When cooked cut in half lengthways. Scoop out and mash the potato flesh. Mix with the tuna, mayonnaise and margarine or butter. Season with salt and pepper and then use this mixture to fill skins. Brown under a hot grill and serve with broccoli or salad.

Vegetable Kebabs
Serves 2

1 small aubergine, halved lengthways and sliced
1 courgette, halved lengthways and sliced thickly
8 medium-sized cap mushrooms
1 small red pepper, deseeded and cut into 8 pieces
2 tablespoons (30ml) olive oil
2 tablespoons (30ml) parsley, chopped
1 teaspoon (5ml) hot red bean and chilli sauce
2 tablespoons (30ml) tomato ketchup

Mix all ingredients together and leave to marinate for 1 hour. Then thread vegetables on to skewers or bamboo sticks. Cook under a hot grill or on a barbecue until vegetables are starting to blacken at edges. Serve with salad and garlic bread.

Curried Egg Salad
Serves 2

3 eggs
3 tablespoons (45ml) salad cream
1 teaspoon (5ml) curry paste
1 tablespoon (15ml) single cream
mixture of lettuce leaves
watercress
sprinkling of paprika
lemon juice

Put the eggs in a small pan and cover with cold water. Bring to the boil and cook for 10 minutes. Immerse eggs in cold water to cool and then remove shells. Meanwhile, mix the salad cream, curry paste and cream together to make a curry sauce. Arrange the lettuce and watercress on plates, sprinkle with the lemon juice. Cut the eggs in half and place 3 halves on each plate (yolk side down). Cover the eggs with the curry sauce. Sprinkle with paprika and serve.

Salmon and Cucumber Salad
Serves 2

> 8-oz (200-g) can pink salmon, drained
> vinegar
> salt and pepper
> pinch of sugar
> half a cucumber
> variety of salad leaves including a red leaf type
> radishes, sliced

Sprinkle some vinegar on the salmon and season with salt and pepper. Put some vinegar into a small bowl with some salt and a pinch of sugar. Cut the cucumber into matchsticks and add to the bowl. Mix well. Leave for 10 minutes. Arrange the salad leaves on plates and divide the salmon into two portions. Place in the middle of each plate and surround with the sliced radish. Wash and drain the cucumber and arrange on the plates. Serve with brown bread rolls and butter.

Sesame Chicken Salad
Serves 2

> 2 chicken breasts, skinned and boned
> 1 tablespoon (15ml) sesame oil
> mixture of baby spinach leaves and watercress
> ⅓ cucumber, sliced
> baby tomatoes, halved
> lemon juice
> black pepper
> 1 tablespoon (15ml) sesame seeds

Brush the chicken with some of the oil and then cook under a medium grill for about 15 minutes, turning frequently. Meanwhile arrange the salad on plates, dress with lemon juice and sprinkle with black pepper. When chicken is cooked, mix rest of oil and sesame seeds together, coat chicken with mixture, and quickly grill again, watching carefully as seeds burn quickly — you want them to be brown, not black! Serve with the salad.

Brown Lentil Salad
Serves 2

 4 oz (100g) brown lentils
 vegetable stock cube
 lettuce leaves
 3 tomatoes, chopped
 ⅓ cucumber, cubed
 half a small onion, finely chopped
 1 tablespoon (15ml) fresh parsley, finely chopped
 French or mustard dressing

Cook the lentils in boiling water to which you have added the vegetable stock cube. They will take 30–40 minutes to cook (see packet for directions). They need to be soft but still retaining their shape. Drain. Arrange the lettuce leaves on plates, mix the tomatoes and cucumber together and place on the plates. Mix the onion and parsley with the drained lentils and dress with your chosen dressing. Add to the plates and serve immediately while lentils are till warm.

Tuna-stuffed Eggs
Serves 2

 3 eggs
 4-oz (100-g) can tuna, drained
 1 tablespoon (15ml) mayonnaise
 dash of Worcester sauce
 variety of salad leaves
 1 carrot, grated
 lemon juice
 black pepper

Put the eggs into a small pan and cover with cold water. Bring to the boil and cook for 10 minutes. Meanwhile mix the tuna, mayonnaise and Worcester sauce together. Arrange the salad leaves and carrot on plates and dress with the lemon juice. When the eggs are cooked, immerse in cold water to cool and then shell. Cut in half lengthways and scoop out the yolk, crumble yolk finely and mix with tuna mayonnaise. Place egg whites on plates (yolk side up) and heap mayonnaise mixture into each half, filling the yolk hole. Sprinkle with black pepper and serve.

Spicy Potato and Tuna Salad
Serves 2

> 8 oz (200g) baby new potatoes
> 8-oz (200-g) can tuna, drained
> 2 tablespoons (30ml) mayonnaise
> 1 teaspoon (5ml) hot red bean chilli sauce
> 2 tablespoons (30ml) single cream
> variety of salad leaves
> ⅓ cucumber, sliced
> 8-oz (200-g) can sweetcorn, drained

Boil a pan of water and place potatoes in it. Cook for 10 minutes. Mix the tuna, mayonnaise, chilli sauce and cream together. Arrange the salad leaves, cucumber and sweetcorn on plates. When potatoes are cooked, drain and smother with tuna dressing. Serve with green salad immediately.

4 Autumn

Season of mists and mellow fruitfulness . . .

This is my favourite time of the year. I love the season whatever the weather is like, but I am especially fond of this time as many of my family's birthdays fall in these months. So with Hallowe'en, Guy Fawkes and the anticipation of Christmas there is plenty to celebrate and Autumn always brings memories of bonfires and parties for me. It's a good time for friends and shared dinners, as the days are fast drawing in and evenings are often cold and damp. This is the time for warming bakes and stuffed vegetable dishes. Fish is excellent at this time of year and, with tasty sauces, makes good, nutritious suppers.

Mackerel in Beer
Serves 2

2 mackerel, cleaned, heads removed
1 onion, sliced
5 fl oz (125ml) beer
5 fl oz (125ml) wine vinegar

Pre-heat oven to 200°C/400°F/Gas 6. Place the fish in a shallow ovenproof dish. Cover with onion and pour in the beer and wine vinegar. Bake in pre-heated oven for 25 minutes. Serve with jacket potatoes and sautéed courgettes.

Sausage Supper
Serves 2

1 onion, chopped
1 oz (25g) margarine
8 oz (200g) potatoes, thinly sliced
8 oz (200g) carrots, thinly sliced
10 fl oz (250ml) stock
4 pork sausages, cooked and thickly sliced
salt and pepper
3 tablespoons (45ml) single cream
1 teaspoon (5ml) mustard
chopped parsley, to garnish

Fry the onion in the margarine until soft. Add potatoes and cook gently for 5 minutes. Add the carrots and stock. Cover and cook for 25 minutes until vegetables are soft. Add the sausages and seasoning and heat through. Just before serving, stir in the cream and mustard and garnish with parsley. Serve with garlic bread.

Mussels with Cider
Serves 2

1½ lb (600g) mussels, cleaned
2 oz (50g) garlic butter
1 small onion, finely chopped
5 fl oz (125ml) medium or dry cider
sprinkling of parsley

Make sure you discard any mussels that have opened. Fry the onion gently in the butter until soft, add the cider and mussels. Cover and cook over a high heat for a few minutes, then check to see if the mussels have opened. If not, cook for another couple of minutes. When the mussels are open, place a sieve over a bowl and collect the juices from the pan. Return the juices to the pan and boil until sauce thickens slightly. Put mussels into serving bowls (discard any that remain shut) and pour juices over. Serve with garlic bread.

Cod in Red Mayonnaise Sauce
Serves 2

1 red pepper
1 tablespoon (15ml) tomato purée
2 oz (50g) ground almonds
4 tablespoons (60ml) mayonnaise
1 tablespoon (15ml) lemon juice
knob of butter
2 cod steaks
black pepper

Put the red pepper in a pre-heated oven at 240°C/475°F/Gas 9 for 15 minutes until skin blackens. Cool, then peel and remove seeds. Blend the flesh with the tomato purée and almonds. Mix in the mayonnaise and lemon juice. Place in a bowl over hot water and leave to heat through. Spread the butter over the cod and season with pepper. Grill under a medium heat for 4 minutes on each side. To serve, pour the sauce onto a plate and place the cod steaks on top. This is nice with new potatoes or rice and a green vegetable.

Aubergine and Tuna Bake
Serves 4

> 2 medium aubergines, sliced
> 4 tablespoons (60ml) oil
> 1 onion, chopped
> 1 tablespoon (15ml) pesto
> 1 tablespoon (15ml) tomato purée
> 14-oz (400-g) can chopped tomatoes
> 14-oz (400-g) can tuna, drained
> 5 fl oz (125ml) Greek yoghurt
> 1 egg, beaten
> 2 oz (50g) Cheddar cheese, grated
> sprinkling of chopped parsley

Pre-heat the oven to 180°C/350°F/Gas 4. In batches, fry the aubergine in half of the oil, remove from pan. Add rest of oil and onion and fry until soft. Add the pesto, tomato purée and tinned tomatoes. Fry for a further 2 minutes. Remove from heat and gently stir in the tuna. Put into a greased lasagne dish. Top with the aubergine. Mix the yoghurt and egg together. Pour over the aubergines and sprinkle with the cheese and parsley. Cook in pre-heated oven for 45 minutes. This is good hot or cold. Serve with jacket potatoes or rice, or garlic bread and salad.

Pesto Pasta
Serves 2

> 8 oz (200g) pasta quills
> knob of butter
> 2 tablespoons (30ml) pesto
> sprinkling of Parmesan cheese

Cook pasta following packet directions. When *al dente*, drain and add butter. When butter has melted, add pesto and stir well. Place in bowls and sprinkle with Parmesan cheese. Serve with garlic bread.

Herby Liver
Serves 2

1 onion, sliced
1 tablespoon (15ml) oil
8 oz (200g) lamb's liver, thinly sliced
1 tablespoon (15ml) tomato purée
1 tablespoon (15ml) Italian herbs
5 fl oz (125ml) stock
2 tomatoes, chopped
sprinkling of chopped parsley

Fry the onion in the oil until soft. Add the liver and cook for 3 minutes, stirring. Add the tomato purée, herbs and stock, mix well. Cover and simmer gently for 20 minutes. Add the tomatoes and heat through. Serve sprinkled with the parsley. This can be served with pasta or rice and peas and carrots.

Veggie Cassoulet
Serves 2

1 onion, sliced
2 cloves garlic, crushed
2 tablespoons (30ml) olive oil
14-oz (400-g) can chopped tomatoes
2 tablespoons (30ml) tomato purée
14-oz (400-g) can haricot beans, drained
8-oz (200-g) can butter beans, drained
4 oz (100g) brown cup mushrooms, quartered
1 tablespoon (15ml) molasses sugar
1 tablespoon (15ml) herbes de Provence
2 tablespoons (30ml) fresh wholemeal breadcrumbs
1 tablespoon (15ml) Parmesan cheese

Pre-heat oven to 180°C/350°F/Gas 4. Fry the onion and garlic in the oil until soft. Put in a greased ovenproof dish with rest of ingredients except breadcrumbs and Parmesan. Mix these two ingredients together and sprinkle over other ingredients. Bake in a pre-heated oven for 45 minutes. Serve with garlic bread.

Lamb Couscous
Serves 2

4 lamb cutlets, fat removed
1 tablespoon (15ml) oil
1 onion, chopped
1 teaspoon (5ml) garlic purée
1 teaspoon (5ml) ginger purée
1 teaspoon (5ml) coriander
1 teaspoon (5ml) cumin
pinch of cinnamon
2 oz (50g) no-need-to-soak prunes, halved
2 oz (50g) no-need-to-soak apricots, halved
8 fl oz (200ml) lamb stock
6 oz (150g) couscous

Brown the chops in the oil. Keep warm whilst frying the onion, garlic, ginger and spices. When onions are soft and taking colour, stir in the prunes, apricots and stock. Bring to the boil, add the lamb, cover and simmer gently for 5 minutes. Meanwhile put the couscous in a bowl, cover with boiling water, and leave for 3 minutes. Drain and break up any lumps that have formed. Put in a metal colander (if the holes are rather large put a piece of muslin or new J-cloth in the bottom). Cover and steam over lamb for 20 minutes. Serve the couscous with the lamb and fruit spooned on top.

Fruity Gammon Steaks
Serves 2

2 gammon steaks
knob of butter
black pepper
4 teaspoons (20ml) fruit chutney

Make little cuts all around the edges of the steaks. Spread butter over steaks and season with pepper. Grill under a medium heat for 5 minutes. Turn over, spread with chutney and grill for 5 minutes. Serve with new or jacket potatoes and peas and sweetcorn.

Fish Creole
Serves 2

>2 white fish fillets
>1 onion, sliced
>1 teaspoon (5ml) garlic purée
>1 green pepper, deseeded and sliced
>1 tablespoon (15ml) oil
>knob of butter
>14-oz (400-g) can chopped tomatoes
>1 tablespoon (15ml) tomato purée
>pinch of molasses sugar
>1 teaspoon (5ml) sweet chilli sauce

Pre-heat oven to 180°C/350°F/Gas 4. Put fish fillets in a greased shallow ovenproof dish. Fry onion, garlic and pepper in oil and butter. Add rest of ingredients and mix well. Spoon over fish and bake in pre-heated oven for 25 minutes. Serve with rice and sautéed courgettes.

Bonfire Bangers
Serves 2

I have always loved Bonfire Night and as we often entertain friends on this night, need a good cheap recipe to make. This is a particular favourite of mine. Our local butcher makes a wide selection of sausages, but if you can't get this variety, use any type that you fancy.

>1 lb (400g) pork and apple sausages
>1 onion, sliced into rings
>1 teaspoon (5ml) oil
>1 tablespoon (15ml) chopped parsley

Grill the sausages under a medium heat, turning occasionally, for 15 minutes. Meanwhile fry the onion rings in the oil, when brown, mix in parsley. When sausages are cooked serve with the onion and parsley. Serve with jacket potatoes and cole-slaw.

Aubergine and Lentil Sauce
Serves 4

1 onion, chopped
1 teaspoon (5ml) garlic purée
1 red pepper, deseeded and chopped
1 green pepper, deseeded and chopped
4 tablespoons (60ml) olive oil
1 aubergine, diced
8 oz (200g) red lentils
10 fl oz (250ml) vegetable stock
14-oz (400-g) can chopped tomatoes
2 tablespoons (30ml) tomato purée
1 tablespoon (15ml) pesto

Fry the onion, garlic and peppers in 2 tablespoons (30ml) of the oil. Add remaining oil and aubergine. Cook for 4 minutes. Add rest of ingredients, bring to the boil and then simmer gently for 20 minutes. Serve with spaghetti or jacket potatoes and salad.

Pasta, Aubergine and Lentil Bake
Serves 2

2 servings of aubergine and lentil sauce (see previous recipe)
6 oz (150g) pasta spirals, cooked
7-oz (200-g) can chopped tomatoes
black pepper
2 tablespoons (30ml) wholemeal breadcrumbs
1 tablespoon (15ml) Parmesan cheese
sprinkling of chopped parsley

Pre-heat oven to 180°C/350°F/Gas 4. Mix together the aubergine and lentil sauce with the pasta and tomatoes, season with pepper. Put in a greased ovenproof dish and cover with breadcrumbs, Parmesan and parsley. Bake in the pre-heated oven for 45 minutes. Serve with garlic bread.

Onion Bake
Serves 4

4 oz (100g) self-raising wholemeal flour
4 oz (100g) strong white flour
2 oz (50g) ground almonds
4 oz (100g) butter
2 tablespoons (30ml) oil
2 onions, chopped
8 oz (200g) fromage frais
3 eggs, beaten
2 tablespoons (30ml) milk
sprinkling of cayenne pepper

Pre-heat oven to 180°C/350°F/Gas 4. Mix together the flours and almonds. Rub in half the butter. Stir in the oil and knead into a smooth dough. Roll out to fit an 8 in (20cm) flan tin. Prick base thoroughly with a fork. Put a layer of greaseproof paper on the base and then some coins to weight it down. Bake in pre-heated oven for 10 minutes. Meanwhile, fry onion in remaining butter. Mix the fromage frais, eggs and milk together. When base is ready, remove greaseproof paper and coins. Spread the onion over the base, pour in fromage frais mixture and sprinkle with cayenne pepper. Continue to bake for a further 35 minutes until golden brown and set. Serve hot with jacket potatoes and broccoli or cold with salad.

Tomato and Courgette Bake
Serves 4

1 lb (400g) tomatoes, sliced
1 lb (400g) courgettes, sliced
4 oz (100g) Mozzarella cheese, grated
1 tablespoon (15ml) fresh basil, chopped
10 fl oz (250ml) whipping cream, slightly whipped
2 tablespoons (30ml) Parmesan cheese, grated

Pre-heat oven to 190°C/375°F/Gas 5. Put the tomatoes, courgettes and Mozzarella in a well greased shallow oven-proof dish. Sprinkle with basil and pour cream over. Sprinkle with Parmesan and bake in pre-heated oven for 35 minutes. Serve hot with new potatoes and broccoli or cold with rice salad and a green salad.

Meatballs and Beans
Serves 2

    1 onion, chopped
    2 cloves garlic, crushed
    4 tablespoons (60ml) oil
    8 oz (200g) mince
    salt and pepper
    sprinkling of parsley
    1 egg, beaten
    14-oz (400-g) can chopped tomatoes
    16-oz (400-g) can baked beans

Fry onion and garlic in oil until soft and starting to colour, remove from pan. Mix mince, salt and pepper, parsley and egg, shape into meatballs and fry until brown. Return onion and garlic to the pan and add rest of ingredients. Simmer for 7 minutes. Serve with garlic bread.

Garlicky Soup
Serves 2

    1 onion, sliced
    2 cloves garlic, crushed
    2 tablespoons (30ml) oil
    14-oz (400-g) can chopped tomatoes
    14-oz (400-g) can red kidney beans, drained
    10 fl oz (250ml) stock
    4 oz (100g) garlic sausage, chopped

Fry the onions and garlic in oil until soft. Add rest of ingredients and bring to the boil. Simmer for 5 minutes. Serve with garlic bread.

Peppery Lamb in Orange Sauce
Serves 2

1 onion, sliced
1 red pepper, deseeded and sliced
1 clove garlic, crushed
2 tablespoons (30ml) oil
2 leg of lamb steaks, thinly sliced
2 teaspoons (10ml) sweet chilli sauce
5 fl oz (125ml) orange juice
2 teaspoons (10ml) cornflour

Fry onion, pepper and garlic in oil until soft. Add lamb and cook for 4 minutes. Mix in chilli sauce. Blend juice with cornflour, add to pan, and bring to boil, stirring. Simmer gently for 2 minutes. Serve with buttered tagliatelle and watercress salad.

Tuna Fishcakes
Serves 2

1 lb (400g) potatoes, cooked and mashed
8-oz (200-g) can tuna, drained
1 tablespoon (15ml) parsley, chopped
salt and pepper
2 tablespoons (30ml) oil
lemon, to garnish

Mix all ingredients, except lemon and oil, together. Shape into four fishcakes. Fry gently in oil for 3–4 minutes, turning once. Serve garnished with lemon, with salad or baked beans.

Courgettes and Mushrooms with Pasta
Serves 2

6 oz (150q) pasta spirals
2 tablespoons (30ml) oil
1 teaspoon (5ml) garlic purée
4 oz (100g) courgettes, sliced
4 oz (100g) mushrooms, sliced
5 fl oz (125ml) stock
1 tablespoon (15ml) pesto
2 tablespoons (30ml) tomato purée
2 tablespoons (30ml) Parmesan cheese

Cook pasta as directed on packet. Whilst cooking, fry garlic, courgettes and mushrooms in oil, add rest of ingredients, except cheese, and bring to the boil. Cover and simmer gently for 5 minutes. Serve mixed into pasta and sprinkled with Parmesan. This is good with watercress salad and garlic bread.

Stuffed Plaice in Mushroom Sauce
Serves 2

1 lemon, grated rind
2 tablespoons (30ml) fresh parsley, chopped
2 oz (50g) fresh wholemeal breadcrumbs
2 plaice fillets, skinned
5-oz (125-g) can condensed cream of mushroom soup
1 tablespoon (15ml) Parmesan cheese

Pre-heat oven to 180°C/350°F/Gas 4. Mix together lemon rind, parsley and breadcrumbs. Divide between the fillets and roll fish up with stuffing inside. Put in a ovenproof dish. Pour the soup over fish, sprinkle with Parmesan and bake in pre-heated oven for 20 minutes. Serve with rice and courgettes.

Smoked Haddock Gratin
Serves 2

> 12 oz (300g) smoked haddock
> 10 fl oz (250ml) milk
> 2 oz (50g) margarine
> 2 oz (50g) flour
> 8 oz (200g) cauliflower florets, cooked
> 4 oz (100g) cheese, grated
> salt and pepper
> 2 oz (50g) butter, softened
> 1 teaspoon (5ml) Dijon mustard
> 8 slices French bread

Pre-heat oven to 190°C/375°F/Gas 5. Put haddock in a pan with milk and bring to the boil, cover and simmer for 6 minutes. Cool and then remove skin and flake fish. Strain the milk. Melt margarine, remove from heat and add flour and a little of the milk, blend well. Return to heat and gradually add rest of milk, stirring continuously. Stir in the cauliflower, cheese and fish, and season. Put into a shallow ovenproof dish. Mix butter and mustard together and spread over bread, place on top of fish, mustard side up. Bake in the pre-heated oven for 25 minutes. Serve with peas.

Tuna Tortilla
Serves 2

> 1 onion, chopped
> 1 clove garlic, crushed
> 1 green pepper, deseeded and chopped
> 4 tablespoons (60ml) oil
> 6 oz (150g) cooked potato, diced
> 8-oz (200-g) can tuna, drained
> 1 tablespoon (15ml) pesto
> 4 eggs, beaten

Cook onion, garlic and pepper in oil until soft. Add potato and cook for a further 5 minutes. Add rest of ingredients. Continue to cook for another 4 minutes until egg has set. Meanwhile pre-heat the grill and finish cooking the tortilla under the grill, so that top browns. Serve in wedges with salad and tomato sauce.

Marrow and Mince Bake
Serves 2

1 marrow, skinned and deseeded, flesh cubed
1 onion, chopped
2 oz (50g) mushrooms, sliced
2 tablespoons (30ml) oil
8 oz (200g) mince
2 tablespoons (60ml) gravy granules
5 fl oz (125ml) hot water
1 tablespoon (15ml) tomato purée
dash of wine
sprinkling of mixed herbs
14-oz (400-g) can chopped tomatoes
1 oz (25g) cheese, grated

Pre-heat oven to 190°C/375°F/Gas 5. Put marrow in greased ovenproof dish. Fry onion and mushroom in oil until soft, transfer to ovenproof dish. Fry mince until brown, make gravy with gravy granules and water, add to pan with tomato purée, wine and herbs. Simmer for 2 minutes. Mix in tomatoes and then transfer to ovenproof dish. Sprinkle with cheese and bake in pre-heated oven for 50 minutes. Serve with garlic bread.

Cheese and Anchovy Tart
Serves 2

> 12 oz (300g) shortcrust pastry (see p 12)
> 1 onion, chopped
> 1 clove garlic, crushed
> 1 oz (25g) butter
> 4 oz (100g) cheese, grated
> 4 eggs, beaten
> 5 fl oz (125ml) double cream
> 5 fl oz (125ml) milk
> 2-oz (50-g) can anchovies, drained
> black pepper

Pre-heat oven to 200°C/400°F/Gas 6. Roll out the pastry to fit an 8 in (20cm) flan tin, prick the base all over with a fork. Put a sheet of greaseproof paper in the bottom and then some coins. Bake in pre-heated oven for 10 minutes. Meanwhile fry onion and garlic in butter. When pastry is ready, remove greaseproof paper and coins. Transfer onion and garlic into flan case. Cover with cheese. Mix together eggs, cream and milk. Pour into case. Top with anchovies and season well. Bake for a further 30 minutes until custard sets and is brown on top. Serve hot or cold with new potatoes and peas or salad.

Lamb with Mint Jelly
Serves 2

> 2 lamb chops
> 1 tablespoon (15ml) mint jelly

Grill chops under a medium grill for about 4 minutes, turn them over and spread with mint jelly. Continue to grill for another 4 minutes. Serve with new potatoes and carrots or peas.

Lamb and Broccoli
Serves 2

1 onion, chopped
1 clove garlic, crushed
2 oz (50g) mushrooms, sliced
2 tablespoons (30ml) oil
1 teaspoon (5ml) molasses sugar
5 fl oz (125ml) stock
sprinkling of rosemary
1 tablespoon (15ml) tomato purée
4 oz (100g) broccoli, divided into small florets
6 oz (150g) cooked lamb, cubed
3 fl oz (75ml) red wine
knob of butter

Fry onion, garlic and mushrooms in oil until soft. Add sugar, stock, rosemary, tomato purée and broccoli. Bring to boil and then simmer for 5 minutes. Add lamb, wine and butter and cook for a further 5 minutes. Serve with buttered pasta or jacket potatoes and salad.

Aubergine and Tomato Gratin
Serves 2

2 aubergines, sliced lengthways
14-oz (400-g) can chopped tomatoes
2 tablespoons (30ml) tomato purée
1 tablespoon (15ml) pesto
1 beefsteak tomato, sliced
4 oz (100g) Mozzarella cheese, sliced
1 tablespoon (15ml) olive oil
black pepper

Pre-heat oven to 180°C/350°F/Gas 4. Put aubergine in a greased, shallow ovenproof dish. Mix together the chopped tomatoes, tomato purée and pesto, spoon over aubergines. Arrange sliced tomato and Mozzarella on top, drizzle with oil and season with black pepper. Bake in pre-heated oven for 35 minutes. Serve with garlic bread and green salad.

Salmon and Broccoli Quiche
Serves 2

> 12 oz (300g) nutty pastry (see p 12)
> 8-oz (200-g) can pink salmon, drained
> 4 oz (100g) broccoli florets, in small pieces
> 2 eggs, beaten
> 3 fl oz (75ml) single cream
> salt and pepper

Pre-heat oven to 200°C/400°F/Gas 6. Line an 8 in (20cm) flan tin with pastry. Prick pastry base all over with a fork. Put some greaseproof paper in the bottom and weigh down with coins. Cook in pre-heated oven for 15 minutes. Remove paper and coins. Spread salmon and broccoli over flan base. Beat together eggs and cream, season, and pour into flan. Bake at 190°C/375°F/Gas 5 for about 20 minutes until filling is set. Serve with salad.

Vegetable Samosas
Serves 2

> 4 oz (100g) potato, cubed
> 4 oz (100g) peas
> 4 oz (100g) self-raising flour
> 2 oz (50g) soft margarine or butter
> sprinkling of curry powder
> salt and pepper
> fat, for frying

Boil potatoes and peas until cooked and soft. Mix the flour and margarine or butter into a dough using some cold water to bind together. Divide mixture into four small balls. Roll out in circles and cut each circle into half. Mix curry powder into potato and pea mixture and place some of mixture in middle of each semi-circle. Wet one corner of dough with water and fold over to form a triangle shape, fold over other side and press edges together to seal. Fry in hot fat for a few minutes to brown all sides. Serve with some mango chutney and salad.

Lamb Hash
Serves 2

  12 oz (300g) cooked lamb, minced
  2 tablespoons (30ml) fresh parsley, chopped
  1 onion, minced
  12 oz (300g) cooked potato, cubed
  8 fl oz (200ml) gravy, made up from packet
  4 fl oz (100ml) tomato ketchup
  1 tablespoon (15ml) oil
  1 oz (25g) cheese, grated

Pre-heat oven to 160°C/325°F/Gas 3. Mix the lamb, parsley, two-thirds of onion, potato, gravy and tomato ketchup together. Put in an uncovered ovenproof dish and cook, stirring occasionally, in oven for 45 minutes. Fry the rest of the onion in the oil until brown. When cooking time is up, sprinkle cheese and fried onion over top of hash and place under a hot grill to melt cheese. Serve with garlic bread.

Curried Cod
Serves 2

  3 tablespoons (45ml) flour
  1 tablespoon (15ml) curry powder
  2 cod fillets
  2 oz (50g) butter
  fresh lemon, to serve

Mix flour and curry powder together and use this mixture to coat cod fillets. Melt butter and fry each fillet for a few minutes on each side until brown and the fish is cooked. (Do not overheat the butter or it will blacken.) Serve cod with some lemon to squeeze over it. Good with new potatoes or rice salad and peas.

Chicken Parmigiana
Serves 2

2 chicken breasts, skinned and boned
8-oz (200-g) can chopped tomatoes
1 tablespoon (15ml) tomato purée
2 teaspoons (10ml) pesto
2 slices aubergine
2 slices Mozzarella cheese
2 tablespoons (30ml) Parmesan cheese

Pre-heat oven to 200°C/400°F/Gas 6. Place chicken in an uncovered ovenproof dish. Mix together the tomatoes, tomato purée and pesto and use to cover chicken. Place an aubergine slice on each chicken breast and then a slice of Mozzarella on this, sprinkle with Parmesan and cook in pre-heated oven for about 45 minutes or until chicken is cooked and cheeses are brown.

Fish in Mushroom Sauce
Serves 2

2 fillets fish (sole or plaice are good)
few slices of onion
3 tablespoons (45ml) dry white wine or fish stock
10 fl oz (250ml) mushroom sauce (see p 9)
parsley, to garnish

Pre-heat oven to 180°C/350°F/Gas 4. Place the fish, onion and wine in a shallow ovenproof dish. Cover and cook in pre-heated oven for 15 minutes. When cooked, carefully remove fish and place on serving plates, pour mushroom sauce over and garnish with parsley. Serve with new potatoes or rice and carrots or a green vegetable.

Marmite and Cheese-stuffed Jackets
Serves 2

2 × 6–8 oz (2 × 150–200g) baking potatoes
oil
2 oz (50g) cheese, grated
1 tablespoon (15ml) soft margarine or butter
Marmite

Pre-heat oven to 200°C/400°F/Gas 6. Brush potatoes with oil and bake in pre-heated oven for 75 minutes. Cut in half lengthways and scoop out potato flesh. Mash together with cheese and margarine or butter. Add Marmite to taste. Pile mixture back into potato jackets and rough up surface with a fork. Cook under a hot grill until potato surface starts to brown. Serve with salad.

Chicken and Mushroom Turnovers
Serves 2

8 oz (200g) flaky pastry
8 oz (200g) cooked chicken, shredded
4 oz (100g) mushrooms, finely chopped
dash of Worcester sauce
10 fl oz (250ml) mushroom sauce (see p 9)
salt and pepper
milk, to glaze

Pre-heat oven to 220°C/425°F/Gas 7. Divide pastry into 2 balls, roll each out into a circle approximately 8 in (20cm) in diameter. Mix together the chicken, mushrooms, Worcester sauce and enough of the mushroom sauce to bind mixture together. Season with salt and pepper. Divide mixture between pastry circles and fold one side over mixture to join the other. Press edges together and crimp edges. Brush with milk and cook on a baking tray in pre-heated oven for 25–30 minutes until pastry is brown and risen. Serve with remaining mushroom sauce (heat through before serving) and broccoli or carrots.

Fish with Ginger
Serves 2

2 fish fillets
1 tablespoon (15ml) oil
1 teaspoon (5ml) garlic purée
1 teaspoon (5ml) ginger purée
1 tablespoon (15ml) soy sauce

Fry the fish gently in the oil for a few minutes on each side. When fish is cooked, transfer to serving plates and quickly stir-fry the garlic, ginger and soy sauce, and pour over fish. Serve with new potatoes or rice and matchstick carrots.

Cod in American Sauce
Serves 2

2 tablespoons (30ml) soft margarine or butter
1 onion, finely chopped
1 clove garlic, crushed
8-oz (200-g) can chopped tomatoes
1 tablespoon (15ml) tomato purée
1 tablespoon (15ml) fresh parsley, chopped
2 teaspoons (10ml) dried tarragon
1 glass dry white wine or fish stock
dash of whisky (optional)
2 cod fillets

In the bottom part of a steamer fry the onion in the margarine or butter until soft. Add all other ingredients except fish, stir well. Put the top part of the steamer on and place fish in this. Cover and cook over a gentle heat for 15 minutes or until fish is cooked. Serve fish with sauce poured over. Good with new potatoes or rice and spinach or other green vegetable.

Vegetable Fritters
Serves 2

10 fl oz (250ml) batter (see p 11)
mixed fresh vegetables, e.g. cauliflower, aubergine
    slices, broccoli, courgette sticks
fat, for frying

Heat the oil until it reaches 190°C/375°F then dip vegetables
in batter and fry for a few minutes until brown and crisp. Serve
with tomato sauce or mango chutney.

Chicken and Banana Kebabs
Serves 2

1 large chicken breast, skinned and boned
2 bananas
1 green pepper, deseeded
2 tablespoons (30ml) oil
1 tablespoon (15ml) mild curry paste
1 tablespoon (15ml) single cream

Cut chicken, bananas and pepper into chunks of a similar
size. Mix with other ingredients and leave to marinate for 1
hour. Thread on to skewers or bamboo sticks. Cook under a
hot grill for 8–10 minutes until chicken is cooked. Serve with
rice, mango chutney and garlic bread.

Tuna and Green Pepper Sauce with Pasta
Serves 2

6 oz (150g) pasta
half a small onion
2 tablespoons (30ml) olive oil
1 green pepper, deseeded and finely chopped
8-oz (200-g) can tuna, drained
5 fl oz (125ml) double cream

Cook pasta as directed on packet. Fry onion in oil with
pepper until soft. Add tuna and cream, stir well and cook until
tuna is warmed through. Drain pasta and serve with tuna.

Pork and Pineapple Curry
Serves 2

12 oz (300g) pork fillet, cubed
1 onion, chopped
2 tablespoons (30ml) oil
1 teaspoon (5ml) garlic purée
1 teaspoon (5ml) ginger purée
2 tablespoons (30ml) curry paste
10 fl oz (250ml) white sauce (see p 9)
sprinkling of sultanas
8-oz (200-g) can pineapple chunks, drained
sprinkling of roasted flaked almonds

Fry the pork and onion in oil until brown. Add garlic, ginger and curry paste and fry gently for a few minutes. Gradually stir in white sauce to make a curry sauce. Add sultanas and pineapple. Stir well and simmer, covered, over a very gentle heat for 20 minutes, stirring occasionally. Serve on a bed of rice, garnished with almonds. Poppadoms are also good with this.

Spanish Pork Chops
Serves 2

1 onion, sliced
1 clove garlic, crushed
1 tablespoon (15ml) olive oil
2 pork chops
2 tablespoons (30ml) flour
1 tablespoon (15ml) paprika
1 red pepper, deseeded and thinly sliced
1 green pepper, deseeded and thinly sliced
14-oz (400-g) can chopped tomatoes

Pre-heat oven to 180°C/350°F/Gas 4. Fry the onion and garlic in the oil until soft, transfer to an ovenproof dish. Coat the pork chops with the flour and paprika and fry for a few minutes on each side. Transfer to ovenproof dish. Cover with the peppers and tomatoes. Cover and cook in pre-heated oven for 75 minutes until meat is tender. Serve with rice.

Vegetable Biryani
Serves 2

 2 tablespoons (30ml) curry paste
 2 teaspoons (10ml) garlic purée
 2 teaspoons (10ml) ginger purée
 8 oz (200g) basmati rice
 3 tablespoons (45ml) oil
 pinch of cumin seeds
 sprinkling of sultanas
 15 fl oz (375ml) boiling vegetable stock
 1 tablespoon (15ml) soft margarine or butter
 1 onion, chopped
 mixture of vegetables e.g. cauliflower florets, courgette
   chunks, carrot sticks, peas
 14-oz (400-g) can chopped tomatoes
 sprinkling of pistachio nuts or almonds

Gently fry half of the curry paste, garlic and ginger with all of
the rice in 1 tablespoon (15ml) of oil. Add the cumin seeds,
sultanas and stock. Stir, then cover and leave to simmer gently
for 20 minutes. Meanwhile gently fry the remaining curry
paste, garlic, ginger and onion in another tablespoon (15ml)
oil and soft margarine or butter. Add vegetables and quickly
stir-fry. Add the tomatoes and simmer gently until rice is
ready. Stir the remaining oil and nuts into the rice, then serve
with vegetable curry. Good with poppadoms and lime
chutney.

Chicken Strogonoff
Serves 2

    1 onion, sliced
    1 tablespoon (15ml) oil
    1 tablespoon (15ml) soft margarine or butter
    12 oz (300g) chicken breast, skinned and boned
    1 tablespoon (15ml) flour
    1 tablespoon (15ml) paprika
    4 oz (100g) mushrooms, sliced
    5 fl oz (125ml) sour cream
    salt and pepper

Fry onion in oil and butter until soft. Cut chicken into strips. Mix together flour, paprika and chicken then fry chicken about 5 minutes until brown. Add mushrooms and quickly stir-fry. Add sour cream and season to taste. When cream has heated through, serve on a bed of rice and peas.

Eggs Florentine
Serves 2

    16 oz (400g) spinach, cooked and puréed
    salt and pepper
    10 fl oz (250ml) cheese sauce (see p 9)
    4 eggs
    grated Parmesan cheese

Pre-heat oven to 190°C/375°F/Gas 5. Season the spinach well and mix with half of the cheese sauce, put in a shallow ovenproof dish. Carefully break the eggs into the dish and then spoon a little sauce over each egg, sprinkle with cheese and bake in pre-heated oven for 15 minutes or until eggs have set. Serve with garlic bread.

Chicken Madras
Serves 2

For those of you who are not curry aficionados, a warning –
Madras curries are hotter than the average curry!

12 oz (300g) chicken meat, skinned
1 tablespoon (15ml) oil
1 tablespoon (15ml) soft margarine or butter
1 onion, chopped
1 teaspoon (5ml) curry powder
1 teaspoon (5ml) chilli powder
2 tablespoons (30ml) tomato purée
pinch of sugar
half a lemon, juice only

Fry the chicken in the oil and butter until brown, add the
onion and cook until soft. Add all other ingredients except
lemon, stir and then cover tightly. Simmer very gently for 30
minutes, stirring occasionally and adding a little water if curry
is looking dry. Add the lemon juice and simmer for another 10
minutes. Serve with rice and a mixture of yoghurt, mint and
cucumber.

Pork Chops with Raisin Sauce
Serves 2

2 pork chops
half a glass of red wine
2 tablespoons (30ml) raisins
8 fl oz (200ml) hot, thick gravy

Cook chops under a medium grill for 4 minutes. Meanwhile
heat together the wine and raisins, mix with the gravy. Turn
chops over, spread a little of gravy on each, and continue to
grill for a further 4 minutes. Serve chops smothered in gravy.
Lovely with new potatoes or chips and mashed swede.

Sausages with Barbecue Sauce
Serves 2

8 oz (200g) sausages
2 oz (50g) soft margarine or butter
small onion, chopped
1 tablespoon (15ml) tomato ketchup
1 tablespoon (15ml) vinegar
1 tablespoon (15ml) brown sugar
1 tablespoon (15ml) Worcester sauce
pinch of mustard

Grill sausages under a medium heat for 15–20 minutes, turning frequently. To make sauce, fry onion in margarine or butter until soft, add rest of ingredients and simmer gently, adding a little water if gets too sticky. Serve sausages with sauce and jacket potatoes and sweetcorn.

Tuna and Corn Pie
Serves 2

1 small onion, chopped
1 tablespoon (15ml) soft margarine or butter
10 fl oz (250ml) parsley sauce (see p 9)
8-oz (200-g) can tuna, drained
8-oz (200-g) can sweetcorn, drained
dash of Worcester sauce
12 oz (300g) cheese pastry (see p 12)
milk to glaze

Pre-heat oven to 200°C/400°F/Gas 6. Fry onion in margarine or butter until soft. Mix with parsley sauce, tuna and sweetcorn. Season with Worcester sauce. Put into a pie dish and cover with a pastry top, using some of the pastry to decorate the top, and crimp the edges. Put a couple of slits in the top of the pastry and brush with milk. Cook in pre-heated oven for 30 minutes until pastry is cooked and brown. Serve with a green vegetable.

5 Winter

Now the days have grown shorter and the cold weather has crept in, it is nice to come home to a hot meal. However, few of us now have the time to produce tender stews and casseroles that have simmered for hours on end. This is possible at the weekend, but not after the daily hassle of returning from a long day at work! Nevertheless, there are many heartening dishes which only take a while to cook – certainly soups come into their own in the winter months. Served with interesting breads and grated cheese or croûtons, soup can make a wonderful supper dish. Spicy foods are also welcome during the cold weather, that warm feeling inside helping to keep winter at bay!

Fruity Indian Chicken
Serves 2

 2 chicken breasts, skinned
 1 tablespoon (15ml) curry paste
 1 tablespoon (15ml) oil
 1 tablespoon (15ml) brown sugar
 1 tablespoon (15ml) lemon or lime juice
 2 tablespoons (30ml) mango chutney
 4 tablespoons (60ml) orange juice

Mix all ingredients, cover and leave to marinate in the fridge for 4–24 hours. Cook the chicken under a medium grill for 20 minutes, turning frequently. The rest of the marinade can be heated to boiling point and then simmered for 2 minutes to make a sauce. Serve with jacket potatoes or rice and a green vegetable.

Goulashy Soup
Serves 2

 1 onion, chopped
 1 teaspoon (5ml) garlic purée
 1 green pepper, deseeded and chopped
 1 tablespoon (15ml) oil
 8 oz (200g) mince
 14-oz (400-g) can chopped tomatoes
 2 tablespoons (30ml) tomato purée
 1 tablespoon (15ml) mixed herbs
 1 tablespoon (15ml) paprika
 15 fl oz (375ml) stock
 sour cream, to garnish

Fry onion, garlic and pepper in oil until soft, add mince and brown. Add rest of ingredients except sour cream, bring to the boil, cover and simmer gently for 15 minutes. Serve garnished with swirls of sour cream and garlic bread.

Sausage and Apple Casserole
Serves 2

1 onion, chopped
1 cooking apple, cored and chopped
2 carrots, diced
2 tablespoons (30ml) oil
4 sausages
1 tablespoon (15ml) parsley, chopped
8 fl oz (200ml) apple juice
2 teaspoons (10ml) cornflour
salt and pepper

Pre-heat oven to 180°C/350°F/Gas 4. Fry onion, apple and carrot in oil until soft. Put in a greased ovenproof dish. Fry the sausages over a gentle heat for 15 minutes, turning occasionally to brown all sides. Put in ovenproof dish. Add parsley and apple juice. Bake in pre-heated oven for 35 minutes. Blend cornflour with a little water and add to dish, mix in, season to taste and cook for a further 10 minutes. Serve with mashed potatoes and a green vegetable.

Pistou Soup
Serves 2

1 onion, chopped
1 clove garlic, crushed
8 oz (200g) carrot, diced
1 green pepper, deseeded and chopped
2 tablespoons (30ml) olive oil
14-oz (400-g) can chopped tomatoes
5 fl oz (125ml) stock
2 oz (50g) small pasta shapes
1 tablespoon (15ml) pesto

Cook onion, garlic, carrot and pepper in oil until soft. Add tomatoes and stock and bring to boil. Cover and simmer for 15 minutes. Add pasta and cook for a further 10 minutes. Just before serving, stir in the pesto. Serve with grated cheese and French bread.

Lamb in Mustard and Rosemary Sauce
Serves 2

1 onion, finely chopped
1 clove garlic, crushed
3 oz (75g) butter
4 small lamb chops
2 teaspoons (10ml) Dijon mustard
sprinkling of rosemary
4 tablespoons (60ml) single cream

Fry onion and garlic in butter until soft, add lamb chops and cook for 5 minutes. Add mustard and rosemary and mix into buttery juices. Add cream, stir well, and heat through. Serve with new potatoes and green beans.

Bobotie
Serves 2

1 slice bread
5 fl oz (125ml) milk
1 onion, chopped
2 cloves garlic, crushed
1 green pepper, deseeded and diced
2 tablespoons (30ml) oil
8 oz (200g) mince
1 tablespoon (15ml) medium curry paste
2 oz (50g) sultanas
2 tablespoons (30ml) mango chutney
1 egg, beaten

Pre-heat oven to 180°C/350°F/Gas 4. Soak the bread in the milk. Fry the onion, garlic and pepper in oil until soft. Add the mince and brown. Stir in the curry paste, sultanas and chutney. Remove the bread from the milk, squeezing out milk, mix bread into mince mixture. Put into a greased ovenproof dish. Beat the egg into the remaining milk and pour over meat mixture. Bake in pre-heated oven for 40 minutes until brown on top. Serve with peas and carrots.

Garlicky Buttered Lentils
Serves 2

1 onion, chopped
2 cloves garlic, crushed
2 tablespoons (30ml) oil
6 oz (150g) green lentils
7-oz (200-g) can chopped tomatoes
10 fl oz (250ml) stock
2 oz (50g) garlic butter
1 tablespoon (15ml) parsley, chopped

Fry onion and garlic in oil until soft, add lentils, tomatoes and stock. Bring to boil, cover and simmer for 25 minutes. Stir in garlic butter and parsley. Serve with French bread and salad.

Thai Pork Curry
Serves 2

2 tablespoons (30ml) Thai curry paste
2 pork steaks, fat removed
1 tablespoon (15ml) lime juice
1 teaspoon (5ml) dried lemon grass
2 tablespoons (30ml) oil
1 onion, chopped
4 oz (100g) creamed coconut, crumbled
6 fl oz (150ml) hot water

Mix the curry paste, pork steaks, lime juice, lemon grass and 1 tablespoon (15ml) oil together, leave to marinate in the fridge for 4–24 hours. Fry the onion in remaining oil until soft. Add the marinated mixture and cook for 5 minutes, stirring. Blend together coconut and water, add to other ingredients and simmer gently for 5 minutes. Serve with rice and chopped fresh tomatoes and green pepper.

Pork Satay
Serves 2

> 2 pork chops, fat removed and cut into cubes
> 4 tablespoons (60ml) soy sauce
> 1 tablespoon (15ml) molasses sugar
> 1 teaspoon (5ml) garlic purée
> 1 teaspoon (5ml) ginger purée
> 4 tablespoons (60ml) peanut butter
> 10 fl oz (250ml) hot water

Mix all ingredients except peanut butter and water. Marinate in the fridge for 4–24 hours. Thread pork onto skewers or satay sticks and grill under a medium heat for 8 minutes, turning once. Meanwhile mix the rest of the marinade mixture with the peanut butter and water and simmer for 4 minutes, stirring. Serve the pork with sauce poured over with rice and peas.

Tomato and Mushroom Bake
Serves 2

> 1 onion, finely chopped
> 4 slices wholemeal bread, crumbled
> 1 tablespoon (15ml) oil
> knob of butter
> 2 oz (50g) chopped mixed nuts
> 1 tablespoon (15ml) chopped parsley
> 14-oz (200-g) can chopped tomatoes
> 6 oz (150) mushrooms, chopped
> salt and pepper

Pre-heat oven to 200°C/400°F/Gas 6. Fry the onion and breadcrumbs in the oil and butter, mix with the nuts and parsley. Mix the tomatoes and mushrooms together and season well. Put half the breadcrumb mixture into a greased ovenproof dish, cover with the tomato and mushrooms, sprinkle over the remaining breadcrumb mixture and bake in pre-heated oven for 30 minutes until brown on top. Serve with a watercress salad.

Bacon and Mushroom Pasta
Serves 2

> 6 oz (150g) pasta
> 6 oz (150g) streaky bacon, rinded and chopped
> knob of butter
> 4 oz (100g) mushrooms, quartered
> 1 tablespoon (15ml) oil
> black pepper
> 2 oz (50g) cheese, grated
> 1 tablespoon (15ml) Parmesan cheese
> sprinkling of fresh parsley, chopped

Cook the pasta as directed on the packet. Whilst cooking, fry the bacon in the butter until starting to crisp. Add mushrooms and continue to cook for 3 minutes. Drain pasta and mix in oil, season well. Put into an ovenproof dish, place bacon and mushrooms on top. Cover with cheese and sprinkle on Parmesan. Cook under a pre-heated hot grill until cheese has melted. Sprinkle with parsley before serving. This goes particularly well with tomato salad.

Cod and Bacon Casserole
Serves 2

> 1 onion, chopped
> 2 oz (50g) bacon, rinded and chopped
> 1 tablespoon (15ml) oil
> 10 oz (250g) cod fillet, skinned
> 14-oz (400-g) can chopped tomatoes
> 1 tablespoon (15ml) tomato purée
> sprinkling of Worcester sauce
> salt and pepper

Pre-heat oven to 180°C/350°F/Gas 4. Fry the onion and bacon in oil until bacon starts to crisp. Mix all ingredients and place in an ovenproof dish. Bake in pre-heated oven for 40 minutes. Serve with jacket or mashed potatoes and green beans or carrots.

Turkey with Mushrooms and Peppers
Serves 2

This recipe is a classic way of using up leftover Christmas turkey – not that we usually have much left after I've fed my family gannets!

> 4 oz (100g) mushrooms, sliced
> 1 green pepper, deseeded and sliced
> 1 tablespoon (15ml) oil
> knob of butter
> 5 fl oz (125ml) white sauce (see p 9)
> dash of Tabasco sauce
> 6 oz (150g) cooked white turkey meat, sliced
> black pepper

Fry the mushrooms and pepper in oil and butter until soft. Add white sauce, Tabasco and turkey, mix well and heat through. Season to taste. Serve with rice.

Lentil and Carrot Lasagne
Serves 2

1 onion, finely chopped
1 teaspoon (5ml) garlic purée
3 oz (75g) carrot, finely chopped
1 tablespoon (15ml) oil
3 oz (75g) green or brown lentils, cooked
14-oz (400-g) can chopped tomatoes
1 tablespoon (15ml) tomato purée
1 tablespoon (15ml) fresh parsley, chopped
salt and pepper
3 oz (75g) lasagne
6 oz (150g) cheese, grated

Pre-heat oven to 200°C/400°F/Gas 6. Fry onion, garlic purée and carrot in oil until soft. Mix with lentils, tomatoes, tomato purée and parsley. Season well. Put a layer of lasagne in a greased ovenproof dish, cover with half the lentil and carrot mixture, sprinkle with one third of the cheese, add another layer of lasagne and the rest of the lentil and carrot mixture, sprinkle with half of the remaining cheese. Finally put a last layer of lasagne on top and sprinkle with remaining cheese. Bake in pre-heated oven for 20 minutes. Serve with a green salad.

Apple-stuffed Mackerel
Serves 2

2 mackerel, cleaned, boned and heads removed
2 oz (50g) parsley and thyme stuffing, made up
1 apple, cored, skinned and diced
knob of butter
10 fl oz (50ml) apple juice

Pre-heat oven to 180°C/350°F/Gas 4. Mix stuffing, apple and butter and stuff mackerel with this mixture. Place in a shallow ovenproof dish and pour apple juice over. Cover and cook in pre-heated oven for 25 minutes. Serve with mashed potato and cauliflower.

Kippers with Orange Butter
Serves 2

2 kippers, heads removed
2 oz (50g) butter, softened
1 tablespoon (15ml) each of rind and juice of 1 orange
black pepper

Cook kippers under a pre-heated medium grill for 8 minutes.
Meanwhile put butter, orange rind and juice into a small pan
and heat. Serve kippers with orange butter poured over them.
Lovely with jacket or new potatoes and peas.

Cod in Coriander Sauce
Serves 2

2 cod steaks or fillets
10 fl oz (250ml) fish stock
1 teaspoon (5ml) coriander
1 oz (25g) butter
2 tablespoons (30ml) double cream

Poach cod in fish stock for 8 minutes, until fish is white and
firm, remove fish and keep warm. Measure 5 fl oz (125ml)
stock into a small pan and boil until reduced by half, add
coriander and whisk in butter. Reduce heat and add cream.
Heat through. Serve cod with sauce poured over. Very good
served with rice and carrots.

Sesame Chicken
Serves 2

1 onion, chopped
1 green pepper, deseeded and sliced
1 tablespoon (15ml) oil
8 oz (200g) cooked chicken, sliced
1 tablespoon (15ml) sesame oil
2 teaspoons (10ml) cornflour
1 tablespoon (15ml) orange juice
dash of soy sauce
1 tablespoon (15ml) sesame seeds

Fry onion and green pepper in oil until soft, add chicken and sesame oil and cook for a further minute, stirring. Blend cornflour and orange juice, add to other ingredients and season with soy sauce. Cook for 1 minute and then add sesame seeds. Mix well. Serve with rice.

Kedgeree
Serves 2

10 oz (250g) fish fillet (smoked haddock or salmon)
1 onion, chopped
1 tablespoon (15ml) oil
knob of butter
2 teaspoons (10ml) curry powder or paste
4 oz (100g) long grain rice
juice of 1 lemon
salt and pepper
1 tablespoon (15ml) fresh parsley, chopped
4 tablespoons (60ml) Greek yoghurt or double cream

Poach the fish in enough water to cover for 8 minutes until flesh is cooked and firm. Reserve cooking liquid. Flake fish. Fry onion in oil and butter, add curry powder or paste, cook for 1 minute. Add rice and then cooking liquid and lemon juice. Simmer until rice is cooked, adding more water if needed. When rice is ready, mix in fish and heat through. Season, stir in parsley and yoghurt or cream. Serve with salad.

Pasta with Mushrooms and Walnuts
Serves 2

6 oz (150g) pasta spirals or bows
1 onion, chopped
1 tablespoon (15ml) oil
knob of butter
4 oz (100g) mushrooms, sliced
2 oz (50g) walnuts, chopped
2 tablespoons (30ml) double cream
salt and pepper

Cook pasta as directed on packet. Whilst pasta is cooking, fry onion in oil and butter until soft and starting to colour. Add mushrooms and cook for a further 3 minutes. Add walnuts and cream and heat through. Season and mix with drained pasta.

Pork Chops with Barbecue Sauce
Serves 2

2 pork chops
1 onion, finely chopped
1 clove garlic, crushed
1 tablespoon (15ml) oil
knob of butter
2 tablespoons (30ml) tomato ketchup
1 tablespoon (15ml) vinegar
1 tablespoon (15ml) honey
dash of soy sauce

Grill chops under a pre-heated medium grill for 10 minutes. Meanwhile, fry onion and garlic in oil and butter until soft and starting to colour. Add other ingredients and heat through. Serve sauce with chops accompanied by jacket potatoes and a green vegetable.

Sausage and Onion Rissoles
Serves 2

8 oz (200g) sausage-meat
1 onion, finely chopped
2 teaspoons (10ml) fresh parsley, chopped
salt and pepper
oil, for frying

Mix the sausage-meat, onion and parsley together, season. Divide into four equal portions. Shape each portion into a flat round cake and fry in a little oil for 5 minutes on each side. Serve with mashed potatoes and baked beans.

Vegetable Goulash
Serves 2

1 onion, chopped
1 teaspoon (5ml) garlic purée
2 tablespoons (30ml) oil
8 oz (200g) potatoes, cubed
8 oz (200g) carrots, cubed
8 oz (200g) courgettes
1 red pepper, deseeded and cubed
14-oz (400-g) can chopped tomatoes
1 tablespoon (15ml) tomato purée
1 tablespoon (15ml) paprika

Fry onion and garlic in oil until soft, add rest of ingredients and bring to boil. Reduce heat and simmer until vegetables are cooked through (approximately 30 minutes). Serve with buttered noodles or brown rice.

Spicy Chicken with Tomatoes and Onion
Serves 2

8 oz (200g) onions, finely chopped
1 clove garlic, crushed
1 tablespoon (15ml) oil
knob of butter
7-oz (200-g) can chopped tomatoes
1 tablespoon (15ml) tomato purée
1 tablespoon (15ml) sweet chilli sauce
2 chicken portions, skinned
2 tablespoons (30ml) cream

Fry the onion and garlic in oil and butter until soft and starting to colour. Add rest of ingredients except cream and stir well. Cover with a tight fitting lid (use a piece of foil to make really tight fitting if necessary), simmer very gently for 45 minutes. Just before serving stir in cream and heat through. Serve with jacket potatoes and a green vegetable.

Devilled Kidneys
Serves 2

1 onion, chopped
1 teaspoon (5ml) garlic purée
1 tablespoon (15ml) oil
knob of butter
4 lambs' kidneys, chopped
8-oz (200-g) can chopped tomatoes
1 tablespoon (15ml) tomato purée
dash of Tabasco sauce

Fry the onion and garlic purée in oil and butter until soft, add kidneys and brown. Add rest of ingredients and bring to the boil. Reduce heat and simmer gently for 10 minutes. Serve with rice and peas.

Stuffed Peppers
Serves 2

> 2 large peppers
> 1 onion, chopped
> 1 tablespoon (15ml) oil
> knob of butter
> 4 oz (100g) mince
> 1 tablespoon (15ml) tomato purée
> 1 tablespoon (15ml) pesto
> 2 oz (50g) cooked rice

Pre-heat oven to 180°C/350°F/Gas 4. Blanch the peppers in boiling water for 1 minute. Allow to cool, slice off the top from each pepper and remove seeds. Fry the onion in oil and butter until soft and starting to colour, add mince and brown. Add other ingredients, mix well and use to stuff peppers. Bake in pre-heated oven for 40 minutes. Serve with a green salad.

Potato Gnocchi with Tomato Sauce
Serves 4

> 1 lb (400g) potatoes, cooked and mashed
> 8 oz (200g) plain flour
> 1 oz (25g) soft margarine or butter
> salt and pepper
> 10 fl oz (250ml) tomato sauce (see p 10)
> 2 teaspoons (10ml) pesto
> Parmesan cheese, to serve

Mix the potato, flour, and margarine or butter together and season well with the salt and pepper. Knead on a floured surface until dough feels elastic. Pull little even-sized pieces of dough off and shape into little rolls, flatten and then twist one end towards you. Cook in boiling salted water for 8–10 minutes (try one to see if it is cooked). Heat the tomato sauce and add pesto. Serve gnocchi with tomato sauce poured over and Parmesan cheese sprinkled on top. Good with garlic bread.

Baked Gnocchi with Mozzarella and Basil
Serves 2

    2 portions gnocchi with tomato sauce (see p 103)
    4 slices Mozzarella cheese
    fresh basil
    black pepper

Pre-heat oven to 190°C/375°F/Gas 5. Put the gnocchi with tomato sauce in an ovenproof dish and cover with sliced Mozzarella. Cut up or chop basil leaves and sprinkle on top of cheese. Season well with black pepper. Bake in pre-heated oven for 30 minutes until cheese has melted and dish has warmed through. Serve with salad and garlic bread.

Chicken and Mushroom Cream Bake
Serves 2

    12 oz (300g) chicken, cooked and shredded
    4 oz (100g) mushrooms, quartered
    10 fl oz (250ml) white sauce (see p 9)
    3 tablespoons (75ml) double cream
    sprinkling of Tabasco sauce
    salt and pepper
    1 tablespoon (15ml) fresh parsley, chopped
    slices French bread, buttered
    sprinkling of paprika

Pre-heat oven to 200°C/400°F/Gas 6. Mix together the chicken, mushrooms, white sauce and cream. Season with Tabasco, salt and pepper and parsley. Put in an ovenproof dish and cover with slices of French bread (buttered side up). Sprinkle with paprika and bake in pre-heated oven for 30 minutes until brown on top. Serve with a green vegetable or carrots.

Turkey and Pepper Stir-fry
Serves 2

This recipe is also ideal for using up cooked turkey.

    1 tablespoon (15ml) oil
    8 oz (200g) turkey breast, skinned
    1 pepper, deseeded and cubed
    8-oz (200-g) can sweetcorn
    2 teaspoons (10ml) ginger purée
    2 tablespoons (30ml) soy sauce
    1 tablespoon (15ml) tomato ketchup
    1 teaspoon (5ml) marmalade
    sesame oil, to serve

Heat the oil in a wok or large frying pan. Stir-fry the turkey and pepper for 3 minutes. Add rest of ingredients and continue to stir whilst cooking for a further 2–3 minutes. Sprinkle with sesame oil just before serving. I think that this is particularly good with noodles – though you may prefer it with rice or even new potatoes.

Steak and Pepper Pasta
Serves 2

Occasionally in the supermarket you will find yourself confronted with a lovely piece of steak with a sticker on it saying it has been 'reduced' to clear. Often it has only been reduced by a few pence, but as this recipe doesn't need much meat, I think that you should take it as a sign that this steak has your name on it!

> 5 oz (125g) pasta
> 1 onion, finely chopped
> 1 tablespoon (15ml) olive oil
> 6 oz (150g) rump steak, cubed
> 10 fl oz (250ml) tomato sauce (see p 10)
> 2 teaspoons (10ml) paprika
> sprinkling of Tabasco sauce
> sprinkling of chopped fresh parsley

Put water on to boil for the pasta. Fry the onion in the oil until browning and soft. Add steak and stir-fry for 2 minutes until brown on all sides. Add tomato sauce and paprika and simmer gently to reduce sauce a little while the pasta is cooking. Just before serving, stir in Tabasco and parsley. Serve with pasta and garlic bread.

Minestrone
Serves 2

1 small onion, chopped
2 oz (50g) streaky bacon, chopped
1 clove garlic, crushed
2 tablespoons (30ml) olive oil
8 oz (200g) mixed vegetables
14-oz (400-g) can chopped tomatoes
14-oz (400-g) can baked beans
15 fl oz (375ml) vegetable or chicken stock
2 oz (50g) pasta
2 tablespoons (30ml) tomato purée
2 teaspoons (10ml) pesto
sprinkling of chopped fresh parsley
Parmesan cheese, to serve

Fry the onion, bacon and garlic in oil until browning. Add vegetables and stir-fry for a few minutes. Add tomatoes and beans and simmer gently. In another pan heat the stock and cook pasta for as long as directed on packet. When pasta is cooked, combine pasta and stock with vegetable mixture. Add tomato purée and pesto, simmer for 5 minutes. Before serving stir in parsley. Serve with Parmesan and garlic bread.

Chicken and Pineapple Chow Mein
Serves 2

4 oz (100g) egg noodles
8 oz (200g) chicken breast, skinned and boned
1 tablespoon (15ml) oil
8-oz (200-g) can pineapple chunks, drained
8-oz (200-g) can bamboo shoots, drained
2 tablespoons (30ml) soy sauce
1 tablespoon (15ml) tomato ketchup
1 tablespoon (15ml) vinegar
1 tablespoon (15ml) runny honey
chilli sauce, to taste
sesame oil, to serve

Put the noodles in a bowl and cover with boiling water. Cut the chicken into bite-sized pieces. Heat the oil in a wok or large frying pan and stir-fry chicken for 2 minutes, add pineapple and bamboo shoots and stir-fry for another 2 minutes. Stir in soy sauce, tomato ketchup, vinegar and honey and coat all ingredients well. Add chilli sauce to taste. Drain noodles and stir into other ingredients. Sprinkle with sesame oil before serving.

Turkey Hash
Serves 2

12 oz (300g) cooked turkey, shredded
12 oz (300g) cooked potato, finely cubed
1 small onion, finely chopped
1 small green pepper, deseeded and finely chopped
2 tablespoons (30ml) turkey dripping or cream
salt and pepper
Tabasco sauce

Pre-heat oven to 180°C/350°F/Gas 4. Bind together the turkey, potato, onion, pepper and dripping or cream. Season well with salt and pepper and add Tabasco to taste. Place in a well greased, shallow ovenproof dish and cook in pre-heated oven for 30–40 minutes until hash is brown. Serve with Brussels sprouts and tomato ketchup or a good chutney.

Haddock Mornay
Serves 2

2 haddock fillets
few slices of onion
glass of dry white wine or fish stock
5 fl oz (125ml) milk
10 fl oz (250ml) cheese sauce (see p 9)
1 oz (25g) soft margarine or butter
2 tablespoons (30ml) single cream
2 oz (50g) cheese, grated

Place the haddock, onion, wine or stock and milk in a large frying pan and bring to simmering point. Cover with foil and then a lid so that steam cannot escape. Cook for 12–15 minutes (depending on thickness of the fillets) then transfer fillets to an ovenproof dish. Use the wine and milk to make the cheese sauce. When sauce is made, add margarine or butter and cream to enrich it. Pour over fish and sprinkle with cheese. Grill under a hot grill for a few minutes until cheese is bubbling and brown. Serve with new potatoes and a green vegetable or simply with toast.

Apple and Stilton-stuffed Jackets
Serves 2

2 × 6–8 oz (2 × 150–200g) baking potatoes
oil
1 apple, cored and cubed
4 oz (100g) Stilton cheese, crumbled
1 tablespoon (15ml) soft margarine or butter
1 tablespoon (15ml) mayonnaise
salt and pepper

Pre-heat oven to 200°C/400°F/Gas 6. Brush potatoes with oil and bake in pre-heated oven for 75 minutes. Cut in half lengthways and scoop out potato flesh, mash with other ingredients and pile back into the potato jacket, rough up surface of potato and grill under a hot grill until potato starts to brown. Serve with salad and garlic bread.

Mince Turnovers
Serves 2

> 8 oz (200g) beef mince
> 1 tablespoon (15ml) oil
> 1 onion, finely chopped
> 1 carrot, finely chopped
> 10 fl oz (150ml) gravy
> salt and pepper
> 8 oz (200g) flaky pastry
> milk, to glaze

Pre-heat oven to 220°C/425°F/Gas 7. Fry the mince in oil until brown, add onion and carrot and cook until soft. Remove from heat and bind together with 1–2 tablespoons (15–30ml) gravy. Season with salt and pepper. Divide pastry into 2 balls. Roll each out into an 8 in (20cm) circle. Divide mixture between circles. Fold one side of circle over the mixture and seal edges, crimping them together. Brush with milk and cook on a baking tray for 25–30 minutes until pastry is brown and risen. Serve with remaining gravy (heated through) and peas or carrots.

Chicken Dopiaza
Serves 2

    2 onions
    2 tablespoons (30ml) oil
    2 teaspoons (10ml) garlic purée
    2 teaspoons (10ml) ginger purée
    12 oz (300g) chicken meat, skinned
    1 tablespoon (15ml) curry paste
    1 tablespoon (15ml) soft margarine or butter
    5 fl oz (125ml) Greek yoghurt
    lemon juice

Cut 1 onion in half lengthways and then cut each half into quarters. Fry onion in 1 tablespoon (15ml) oil with half of garlic and ginger purée, and all of chicken. Finely chop other onion and in another pan heat rest of oil with remaining onion, garlic and ginger purée, curry paste and margarine or butter. Add yoghurt and lemon juice to taste; do not let this mixture boil. When chicken is cooked (test with a sharp knife – when juices run clear it is done) pour sauce over chicken and serve with rice and poppadoms.

Pasta with Anchovy and Garlic Sauce
Serves 2

    6 oz (150g) pasta
    5 fl oz (125ml) double cream
    2 oz (50g) butter
    2-oz (50-g) can anchovy fillets, drained
    black pepper
    sprinkling of chopped fresh parsley

Cook pasta as directed on packet. Bring cream to boil and then simmer gently for 5 minutes. Chop anchovies and fry in butter, squashing them down as stirring. Gradually stir in cream. When pasta is cooked, drain and mix with sauce, season with black pepper and serve sprinkled with parsley.

Turkey and Chestnut Turnovers
Serves 2

Although I have included several recipes in this chapter that will help when you have run out of ideas for what to do with the turkey from the Christmas dinner, I think this recipe is the best.

8 oz (200g) flaky pastry
8 oz (200g) cooked turkey, shredded
3 oz (100g) chestnuts, cooked
2 oz (50g) cooked stuffing
10 fl oz (250ml) parsley sauce (see p 9)
salt and pepper
Tabasco sauce
milk, to glaze

Pre-heat oven to 220°C/425°F/Gas 7. Divide pastry into 2 balls. Roll each into an 8 in (20cm) circle. Bind together the turkey, chestnuts and stuffing using some of the sauce. Season with salt and pepper and Tabasco sauce to taste. Divide mixture between pastry circles. Turn one side of circle over mixture and seal the edges, crimping together. Brush with milk and cook on a baking tray for 25–30 minutes until pastry is cooked and risen. Serve with the rest of the sauce (heated through) and Brussels sprouts or carrots.

Fish Balls in Tomato Sauce
Serves 2

You can buy minced fish from most fish counters at super-markets. However, if you cannot get it, it is a simple matter to mince up your own — just buy slightly more to allow for wastage. A very good result comes from mixing mackerel and cod or coley.

16 oz (400g) minced fish
2 oz (50g) flour
1 oz (25g) soft margarine or butter
salt and pepper
10 fl oz (250ml) tomato sauce (see p 10)

Mix together all ingredients except sauce. Shape into little balls. Heat sauce and add fishballs, cover and simmer very gently for 15 minutes. Serve with garlic bread.

Venison with Rowan Mustard
Serves 2

2 venison steaks
2 tablespoons (30ml) rowan jelly
1 tablespoon (15ml) wholegrain mustard

Cook venison under a medium grill for 6 minutes. Turn over and divide half of rowan jelly between the steaks, spreading it over the steak surface. Continue to grill for 5 minutes until meat is cooked. Mix the rest of the jelly with mustard and serve this with the meat. This is good with mashed potatoes or swede and peas.

Turkey and Avocado Kebabs
Serves 2

> 8 oz (200g) turkey breast, skinned and boned
> 1 avocado, stoned and peeled
> 1 tablespoon (15ml) olive oil
> 1 tablespoon (15ml) lemon juice
> 1 tablespoon (15ml) pesto

Cut turkey and avocado into same size pieces and mix with other ingredients. Leave to marinate for 1 hour. Thread onto skewers or bamboo sticks and cook under a hot grill for 10 minutes. Serve with a tomato salad and garlic bread.

6 Vegetables

There has been increased interest in vegetables and vegetarian cooking in the past years. Vegetarians are now not seen as the cranks they were once thought of. Instead, vegetables are seen as an increasingly important part of our diet and it is recommended that they are eaten every day in some form or other. Although as a child the only vegetables that I could be persuaded to eat were potatoes and peas, I now enjoy all types of vegetables.

When you are first learning to cook, fresh vegetables can pose a problem. The cheapest way to buy them is unpacked (and the most environmentally friendly way!) and when bought this way, there are no instructions on how to cook them. As many people now do not learn how to cook before they leave home, many vegetables which were once commonly used are no longer bought – as people do not know how to prepare and cook them. This is a great shame as often these are the very vegetables which are cheap to use. Therefore, this chapter is a guide to preparing and cooking vegetables to accompany your supper dish.

Asparagus (sprue)

Native asparagus comes into season in mid-Spring, and after a few weeks can be bought in bundles from market stalls at very reasonable prices (often cheaper than broccoli at a supermarket!). Sprue is much thinner than the thick asparagus spears, but just as tasty. It is important to wash the spears very thoroughly or you will end up with a gritty vegetable dish. You will need to cut off the woody stem before cooking. Some people prefer to remove the white part of the stem, others scrape it to ensure it is not stringy. Assuming that you don't have a special upright pan for cooking asparagus, you will need some string and a piece of foil. Tie the asparagus in a bundle, buds pointing upwards. Cover the buds in a tight ball of foil. To cook, place the stems in a pan of boiling water.

Boil: 10 minutes
Serve: 8 stems per person

Aubergine

These can be bought all through the year but are usually at their cheapest in the autumn months. They can be stuffed with rice mixtures as a main course, or fried and served as an accompaniment. (Beware – they can absorb a lot of oil which makes them very calorific.) To prepare, cut off the stem and little leaves. Slice or cut into small chunks, if deep frying. Make sure the oil is hot before frying a few slices at a time.

Fry: 4 minutes
Serve: 6 oz (150g) per person

Avocado

Avocado is very good either mashed and served with spicy dishes, such as chilli, or sliced or cubed in salads. Do not use avocados that are very squashy, look for ones that give when pressed with your thumb. If you are buying the avocado a few days before using, choose one that is still hard and ripen it by putting in a brown bag with a ripe banana and leaving them together. To serve, cut the avocado in half lengthways, cut around the stone, pull the two halves apart and remove the stone. Peel the skin off and either mash with a little garlic and lemon juice or slice or cut into cubes to use in salads. The flesh discolours quite rapidly so sprinkle with lemon juice if not using immediately.

Broad beans

These come into season at the end of Spring. Split the shell and remove the beans. Place in boiling water. Beware of using them late in the season as they can become quite tough.

Boil: 15 minutes
Serve: 8 oz (200g) per person – weight as bought

Broccoli

Broccoli is at its best in the winter months. Although it can be eaten raw, it is best lightly cooked. To prepare, cut off the end of the stem and remove any side leaves. If the florets are particularly large you may have to divide them up. Cook in a pan of boiling water.

Boil: 8 minutes
Steam: 6 minutes
Serve: 6 oz (150g) per person

Brussels sprouts

These are in season in the autumn and winter months (there is an old saying that they are not at their best until touched by frosts). Usually served cooked in boiling water, but can also be quartered and used in stir-fries. Discard any discoloured or loose leaves. Do not cut a cross in the bottom of the stem (this used to be suggested, but makes them go mushy).

Boil: 10 minutes
Steam: 8 minutes
Serve: 4 oz (100g) per person

Cabbage

Available in some form throughout the year, cabbage is a much abused vegetable and really deserves to be used more often. The trick is not to overcook it as it becomes mushy and reminiscent of school dinners!

In winter the hearted varieties such as Savoy are very good. To prepare, remove outer leaves. Quarter the heart and shred thinly. Wash well, leaving water on leaves and put into a pan with a large knob of butter. Cover and bring to boil, before leaving to simmer. The only difference when preparing the loose leaf spring greens is to remove stalks, pile the leaves together and then shred before washing.

Simmer: 5 minutes
Steam: 4 minutes
Serve: 6 oz (150g) per person

Carrots

Carrots are a mainstay vegetable, available throughout the year and always cheap. Baby spring carrots are lovely cooked whole, whilst older carrots should have their tops cut off, be peeled and then cut into matchsticks or sliced.

WHOLE BABY CARROTS

Boil: 12 minutes
Steam: 16 minutes
Serve: 6 oz (150g) per person

OLD CARROTS

Boil: 8 minutes
Steam: 12 minutes
Serve: 4 oz (100g) per person

Cauliflower

Cauliflower is another vegetable that is available throughout the year. However, it is at its cheapest and its best in the late summer and early autumn months. It is one of those vegetables that can be much cheaper from a marketstall than the supermarket. This is because the supermarkets demand unblemished produce, so often cauliflowers that don't quite make the grade required by the supermarkets end up being sold by market traders at a very fair price. It is easy to prepare – cut off the end of the woody stem, divide into florets and preferably steam. Cauliflower is often served with a cheese sauce.

Boil: 8 minutes
Steam: 5 minutes
Serve: 6 oz (150g) per person

Celeriac

This is one of those vegetables that it took me quite a while to discover. It is not so commonly available as some, but well worth discovering. It is at its best and most commonly available from late autumn to early winter. To prepare, peel fairly thickly, cube and cook in boiling water before mashing with butter. It can also be sliced and steamed before serving with melted butter.

Boil: 15 minutes
Steam: 20 minutes
Serve: 8 oz (200g) per person

Courgettes

These are probably my favourite vegetable. They are very versatile and can be eaten raw in salads, either cut into matchsticks or grated, or steamed or sautéed. They are also commonly stuffed and baked as a main course dish. To prepare, just cut off the stalk end and cut into matchsticks or rings if steaming; cut into chunks if sautéing.

Steam: 5 minutes
Sauté: 5 minutes
Serve: 4 oz (100g) per person

Fennel

Fennel has an unusual taste, reminiscent of aniseed and is a popular accompaniment to fish. I much prefer it steamed rather than boiled; it is also very good baked in a tomato sauce. To prepare, trim and cut into lengths.

Steam: 12 minutes
Serve: 1 bulb per person

French beans

During the summer I cook a great deal of French beans. They have a better flavour than runner beans and seem to go so well with many dishes. I also like their bright green colour when cooked. When really young they need no preparation. Otherwise just top and tail them – you should cook them whole. Again I prefer them steamed, but you can boil them successfully.

Boil: 8 minutes
Steam: 8 minutes
Serve: 4 oz (100g) per person

Jerusalem artichokes

These can be a pain to prepare – try to avoid the knobbliest specimens. They should be available throughout the winter months. They are peeled, halved if large and then cooked in boiling water to which some lemon juice must be added to avoid discolouring. Serve with plenty of melted butter or a cheese sauce.

Boil: 15–20 minutes
Serve: 6 oz (150g) per person

Leeks

These are extremely popular during the autumn and winter months and are usually served coated with white sauce. An alternative is to fry them for a few minutes in butter and when cooked add a little cream, or fry in oil with garlic and add some tomato purée. To prepare, cut off the tops and roots, removing any coarse outer leaves. Wash thoroughly, squeezing gently, as grit can hide within the leaves. Slice thinly if frying, thickly if serving with white sauce.

Steam: 10 minutes
Fry: 4–5 minutes
Serve: 1 leek per person

Mangetout

Widely available from the end of spring, these are absolutely delicious. To prepare, you only have to top and tail them. They are so easily over-cooked, I much prefer them steamed.

Steam: 6 minutes
Serve: 8 oz (200g) per person, bought weight

Mushrooms

Mushrooms can make a good accompaniment to plain fried or grilled meat. Choose closed cap mushrooms. They should not be washed but just wiped. Cut the end of the stalk off. Melt a knob of butter in a small pan and put mushrooms in stalks uppermost, add a squeeze of lemon. Cover and cook, shaking gently once or twice.

Fry: 4 minutes
Serve: 4 oz (100g) per person

Onions

Although onions are commonly used within cooked dishes, they can also be used as an accompanying vegetable dish. I particularly like them glazed. This can be done with whole button onions or large sliced onions. To prepare, peel and remove the roots. If a large onion, halve and slice, if button onions leave whole. Heat a large knob of butter with the onions and one tablespoon (15ml) sugar. Cook until soft and very brown.

Fry: 4–5 minutes
Serve: 4 oz (100g) per person

Parsnips

Again, a vegetable that is widely used in the autumn and winter months. Parsnips are lovely par-boiled and roasted, but they can also be served sliced or mashed. To prepare, cut off the top and peel. Cut into slices and cook in boiling water. If serving mashed, when cooked, mash or purée with butter and black pepper.

Boil: 20 minutes
Roast: 45–60 minutes
Serve: 8 oz (200g) per person

Peas

Fresh peas are sublime. The season is very short, so if you do see some, buy them up immediately. If you do get some and you have a garden (and some fine weather!) I suggest you take an ice cold drink outside and shell them, remembering that this is how one had to do the vegetables before freezers were invented. Peas are easy to prepare: split each pod and hold over a basin, run your nail down the pod, shelling the peas into the basin. Place in boiling water with a pinch of sugar and a sprig of mint.

Boil: 8–10 minutes
Serve: 8 oz (200g) per person, bought weight

Potatoes

These must be the most versatile of vegetables. Personally I prefer new potatoes served with melted butter and a sprinkling of herbs. However, you can also mash potatoes, bake them in their jackets, roast or chip them. You can also par-boil them and then fry in some hot butter for sauté potatoes, or par-boil them, grate and then fry them made into little cakes called *rosti*. In fact you could probably write another book on the many and various ways of cooking potatoes. Therefore I will just give the most common ways here.

NEW POTATOES

Do not peel. If they are the loose-skinned type, scrape. If you have any larger specimens, cut in half. Cook in boiling water.

Boil: 15 minutes
Serve: 6 oz (150g) per person

JACKET POTATOES

Do not peel. Choose even-sized potatoes. Wash skins and rub with oil. Bake in a pre-heated oven at 200°C/400°F/Gas 6.

Bake: 75 minutes
Serve: 8 oz (200g) potato per person

MASHED POTATOES

Use old potatoes. Peel, quarter and cook in boiling water. Drain and mash with butter and a little milk.

Boil: 20 minutes
Serve: 8 oz (200g) per person

CHIPS

Although something one shouldn't have too often, it is nice to indulge occasionally. Peel old potatoes and cut into slices and then cut the slices into strips. Wash and then dry well. Cook in a pre-heated deep fat fryer at 190°C/375°F. Dry on kitchen paper before serving.

Fry: 8 minutes
Serve: 6 oz (150g) per person

Pumpkin

Pumpkin is a lovely vegetable available in the autumn months. It is easy to prepare and should be mashed and seasoned well or cubed and served with cheese sauce. It can be bought either whole (if small enough) or by the piece if from a large specimen. To prepare, peel, remove seeds and cube flesh. Boil until cooked, then serve with cheese sauce poured over or mash, season with black pepper, butter and a tablespoon of cream.

Boil: 10–15 minutes
Serve: 8 oz (200g) per person

Runner beans

From mid-summer onwards, runner beans are both good and plentiful, and often extremely cheap. To prepare, top, tail and if necessary remove any fibrous strings from the sides (there are now many stringless varieties). Slice into lengths approximately 1 inch (2.5cm) long. Cook in boiling water.

Boil: 8 minutes
Serve: 4 oz (100g) per person

Spinach

When young, spinach leaves can be used whole in salads and dressed with lemon and yoghurt. The larger the leaf, the tougher it gets and it should then be cooked and served with butter, or cooked, sieved and mixed with melted butter and a tablespoon of cream. To prepare, wash well and strip off any large stalks. Do not shake the excess water from the leaves but put into a saucepan, cover, bring to the boil and then cook gently.

Simmer: 8–10 minutes
Serve: 8 oz (200g) per person

Swede

Another vegetable that is popular in the autumn and winter months. Swede can be cooked and served in cubes or slices with melted butter or cheese sauce or it can be mashed. It is often mixed with mashed potato. To prepare, it should be thickly peeled and then cubed or sliced. Cook in boiling water.

Boil: 20 minutes
Serve: 6 oz (150g) per person

Turnips

I have never been a fan of turnips when they are old as I find that they are often hollow and woody. However, baby turnips are absolutely wonderful and I always serve them glazed. Baby turnips do not need peeling, just remove the top and thinly slice. Fry in a knob of butter with a tablespoon (15ml) sugar and a tablespoon (15ml) stock or fruit juice.

Fry: 6 minutes
Serve: 4 oz (100g) per person

7 Desserts and Cakes

In our house we tend to finish our meals with a piece of fruit, a yoghurt or ice cream. However, once a week I do tend to make some sort of dessert or cake that keeps us going for a few days.

I never used to be very keen on baking cakes but that changed when I met and married a fanatical cricketer – the problem with going out with cricketers is that inevitably it will come round to being your turn to make the cricket tea. However, I must admit that they are very appreciative of home-baked cakes so they do make you feel that it was worthwhile going to all that trouble. I have also discovered that it really is useful to have an electric beater – with one of these gadgets, cake-making really is a much simpler chore and I admit that I quite enjoy baking now!

So here is a collection of the cakes and desserts that I tend to make in the course of the year. You will notice that fruit plays a large part – this is because we grow some ourselves and also live in an area where there are many fruit farms. I particularly enjoy going out to pick some fruit and then being able to transform it into lovely tarts and cakes. You will find that if you live near a market there are certain times of the year when the traders are almost giving fruit away – this is the time to start baking.

Rhubarb and Almond Cake

    8 oz (200g) soft margarine
    6 oz (150g) sugar
    pinch salt
    2 eggs, beaten
    8 oz (200g) plain flour
    1 teaspoon (5ml) baking powder
    3 oz (75g) cornflour
    3 oz (75g) ground almonds
    1 lb (400g) rhubarb, cleaned and chopped
    1 tablespoon (15ml) preserving sugar

Pre-heat oven to 180°C/350°F/Gas 4. Beat half of margarine with 4 oz (100g) of sugar, add salt and then eggs. Mix the flour with the baking powder and half of the cornflour, stir gently into the creamed mixture, add half of the ground almonds. Grease a 9 in (23cm) tin and line with greaseproof paper. Put cake mixture in, smooth top and place rhubarb on top. Rub together remaining ingredients except preserving sugar. Spread crumble mixture over rhubarb and then sprinkle with preserving sugar. Bake in pre-heated oven for 70–75 minutes.

Lemon Cake

    4 oz (100g) soft margarine
    8 oz (200g) caster sugar
    2 eggs, beaten
    4 oz (100g) self-raising flour
    rind and juice of lemon

Pre-heat oven to 180°C/350°F/Gas 4. Beat the margarine with half the sugar. Beat in the eggs and then gently stir in the flour and the lemon rind. Put in a greased and lined 8 in (20cm) cake tin and bake in pre-heated oven for 40 minutes. Remove cake to a wire rack. Mix remaining sugar with lemon juice and spoon over top of cake. As cake cools this will form a sugar crust.

Rhubarb Charlotte

   1 lb (400g) rhubarb, cleaned and cubed
   3 oz (75g) unsalted butter
   6 oz (150g) fresh wholemeal breadcrumbs
   1 teaspoon (5ml) mixed spice
   2 oz (50g) brown sugar
   2 tablespoons (30ml) orange juice
   2 tablespoons (30ml) runny honey

Pre-heat oven to 200°C/400°F/Gas 6. Fry the rhubarb gently in half of the butter until soft. Remove from the pan. Fry the breadcrumbs in remaining butter until butter is absorbed and breadcrumbs are brown. Layer the rhubarb and breadcrumbs into an ovenproof dish, finishing with a layer of breadcrumbs. Mix rest of ingredients together and spoon over breadcrumbs. Bake in pre-heated oven for 20 minutes or until top is brown.

Note
You can also make **Blackberry Charlotte** by replacing the rhubarb with 1 lb (400g) blackberries. As you do not need to fry the blackberries you will only need half the amount of butter.

Strawberry Tart

   12 oz (300g) shortcrust pastry (see p 12)
   2 tablespoons (30ml) strawberry jam
   12 oz (300g) strawberries, hulled and halved
   1 tablespoon (15ml) redcurrant jelly

Pre-heat oven to 220°C/425°F/Gas 7. Roll out pastry to fit an 8 in (20cm) pie plate. Spread with jam and cover with strawberries (skin side up). Bake in pre-heated oven for 30 minutes. Melt redcurrant jelly and use to glaze tart.

Note
Try substituting a mixture of tayberries, loganberries and blueberries for the strawberries – absolute heaven.

Honey Cake

6 oz (150g) soft margarine
8 tablespoons (120ml) golden syrup
2 eggs, beaten
4 tablespoons (60ml) marmalade
4 tablespoons (60ml) runny honey
12 oz (300g) self-raising flour
1 teaspoon (5ml)
baking powder
2 teaspoons (10ml) allspice
5 fl oz (125ml) milk
2 oz (50g) cornflakes, crumbled

Pre-heat oven to 180°C/350°F/Gas 4. Beat together the margarine, 6 tablespoons (90ml) golden syrup and the eggs. Beat in half of the marmalade and half of the honey. Sift together the flour, baking powder and allspice, fold into cake mixture, using enough of the milk to get a dropping consistency. Put into a greased and lined 8 in (20cm) cake tin. Level top. Mix remaining syrup, honey and marmalade with cornflakes and spread over surface of cake. Bake in pre-heated oven for 1 hour, until cake is firm to the touch.

French Apple Tart

8 oz (200g) puff pastry
5-oz (125-g) can apple sauce
4 Granny Smith apples, peeled, cored and thinly sliced
knob of butter
1 tablespoon (15ml) caster sugar
2 tablespoons (30ml) apricot jam

Pre-heat oven to 230°C/450°F/Gas 8. Roll out pastry to fit a 8 in (20cm) pie tin. Spread with apple sauce. Arrange apple slices in concentric overlapping rings. Dot with butter and sprinkle with sugar. Bake in pre-heated oven for 15 minutes or until pastry is golden brown and crisp and edges of apple are slightly brown. Melt apricot jam and use to glaze.

Lemon Curd Lattice Tart

1 lb (400g) shortcrust pastry (see p 12)
4 tablespoons (60ml) lemon curd
milk, for glazing
1 tablespoon (15ml) caster sugar

Pre-heat oven to 220°C/425°F/Gas 7. Roll out two thirds of pastry to fit a 8 in (20cm) pie dish. Spread with lemon curd. Roll out rest of pastry to a rectangle 8× 4 in (20×10cm). Cut lengthways into 8 strips. Place 4 strips at equal distances apart across the tart filling. Arrange the other 4 strips at an angle to the first and crossing over the first 4 strips. Glaze with milk and sprinkle with sugar. Bake in pre-heated oven for 30 minutes or until pastry is brown and crisp.

Bakewell Tart

12 oz (300g) shortcrust pastry (see p 12)
2 tablespoons (30ml) raspberry jam
6 oz (150g) soft brown sugar
6 oz (150g) soft margarine
3 eggs, beaten
3 oz (75g) ground almonds
6 oz (150g) sponge cake, crumbled
2 tablespoons (30ml) flaked almonds

Pre-heat oven to 180°C/350°F/Gas 4. Roll out pastry to fit an 8 in (20cm) pie dish. Spread with jam. Beat together sugar and margarine, beat in eggs. Stir in ground almonds and cake crumbs. Spoon mixture over jam. Sprinkle with flaked almonds. Bake in pre-heated oven for 40 minutes until brown on top and well risen.

Lemon Meringue Pie

12 oz (300g) shortcrust pastry (see p 12)
3 tablespoons (45ml) cornflour
5 fl oz (125ml) water
grated rind and juice of 2 lemons
7 oz (175g) caster sugar
2 eggs, separated

Pre-heat oven to 220°C/425°F/Gas 7. Roll out pastry to fit an 8 in (20cm) pie dish. Place a sheet of greaseproof paper inside and some coins. Bake in a pre-heated oven for 15 minutes. Remove paper and coins. Blend together the cornflour and water, put into a small pan with lemon rind and juice and bring to boil, stirring. Reduce heat and add 4 oz (100g) sugar. When sugar has dissolved remove from heat and cool slightly. Beat the egg yolks and add to lemon mixture. Spoon into pastry case. Beat egg whites with half of remaining sugar. When stiff fold in rest of sugar and pile meringue on to lemon filling. Bake in the oven for 10-15 minutes until meringue crisp and lightly browned.

Note
To make **Key Lime Pie** replace the pastry base with a base made with 3 oz (75g) melted butter and 6 oz (150g) digestive or ginger snap biscuit crumbs mixed together and chilled instead of cooked. Replace the 2 lemons with 2 limes.

Baked Sultana Cheesecake

8 oz (200g) shortcrust pastry (see p 12)
1 lb (400g) curd cheese
5 fl oz (125ml) natural yoghurt
2 eggs, beaten
3 oz (75g) caster sugar
2 tablespoons (30ml) cornflour
grated rind of 2 lemons and 1 tablespoon (15ml) juice
4 oz (100g) sultanas

Pre-heat oven to 180°C/350°F/Gas 4. Roll out pastry to line the bottom inch (2.5cm) of an 8 in (20cm) deep cake tin. Beat together the cheese, yoghurt, eggs, caster sugar, cornflour, lemon juice and half of grated lemon rind. Sprinkle sultanas and rest of lemon rind into pastry base. Pour cheese mixture over and bake in pre-heated oven for 35 minutes. Turn off oven, but do not remove cheesecake until cold.

Almond Slices

8 oz (200g) self-raising flour
4 oz (100g) sugar
1 teaspoon (5ml) ground cinnamon
6 oz (150g) unsalted butter
1 egg, beaten
2 oz (50g) flaked almonds
1 oz (25g) preserving sugar

Pre-heat oven to 190°C/375°F/Gas 5. Sift flour, sugar and cinnamon into a bowl and mix with butter until you have a crumb mixture. Add 1 tablespoon (15ml) egg and knead to a dough. Roll out to fit a 11×7 in (28×18cm) tin. Brush with egg and sprinkle with flaked almonds and sugar. Bake in pre-heated oven for 25–30 minutes. Cool for 5 minutes then cut into 12 slices.

Apricot Cheesecake

    12 oz (300g) gingernuts, crushed
    6 oz (150g) butter, melted
    2 teaspoons (10ml) powdered gelatine
    3 tablespoons (45ml) water
    12 oz (300g) cream cheese
    5 fl oz (125ml) whipping cream, whipped
    5 fl oz (125ml) apricot yoghurt
    8 oz (200g) apricots, stoned and halved
    1 tablespoon (15ml) apricot jam

Mix together gingernut crumbs and butter, use to line the base of an 8 in (20cm) springform tin. Chill. Sprinkle gelatine into water and leave to swell, then set over a pan of hot water and stir until it dissolves. Beat together the cream cheese, cream and yoghurt, mix in gelatine mixture and blend well. Pour into base. Chill until it sets. Remove from tin and decorate with apricots. Melt jam and use to glaze fruit.

Raspberry and Almond Cake

    6 oz (150g) soft margarine
    6 oz (150g) caster sugar
    6 oz (150g) ground almonds
    6 oz (150g) self-raising flour
    1 teaspoon (5ml) baking powder
    1 teaspoon (5ml) ground cinnamon
    8 oz (200g) fresh raspberries
    1 tablespoon (15ml) preserving sugar

Pre-heat oven to 180°C/350°F/Gas 4. Beat together 4 oz (100g) each of margarine, sugar and almonds with all the flour, baking powder and cinnamon. Put into a greased and lined 8 in (20cm) springform tin. Cover with raspberries. Rub together the remaining margarine, sugar and almonds, sprinkle over raspberries and then sprinkle with preserving sugar. Bake in pre-heated oven for 1 hour.

Apple Cake

8 oz (200g) cooking apples, peeled, cored and
  chopped
8 oz (200g) mixed dried fruit
6 oz (150g) soft brown sugar
5 fl oz (125ml) Guinness
12 oz (300g) self-raising flour
1 tablespoon (15ml) mixed spice
6 oz (150g) soft margarine
1 egg, beaten
1 tablespoon (15ml) preserving sugar

Mix the apples with the dried fruit, brown sugar and Guinness. Stand overnight. Pre-heat oven to 160°C/325°F/Gas 3. Sift the flour and spice together and rub in the margarine. Stir into the apple mixture with the egg. Put into a greased and lined 8 in (20cm), deep cake tin. Sprinkle with preserving sugar. Bake in pre-heated oven for 90 minutes.

Country Cake

6 oz (150g) soft margarine
3 oz (75g) soft brown sugar
3 eggs, beaten
4 tablespoons (60ml) runny honey
9 oz (225g) wholemeal self-raising flour
1 teaspoon (5ml) baking powder
1 teaspoon (5ml) cinnamon
2 oz (50g) chopped mixed nuts
4 oz (100g) cream cheese
2 oz (50g) icing sugar
2 teaspoons (10ml) coffee essence
sprinkling of toasted mixed nuts

Pre-heat oven to 180°C/350°F/Gas 4. Beat together all ingredients except cream cheese, icing sugar, coffee essence and toasted mixed nuts. Put in a greased, lined 8 in (20cm), deep cake tin. Bake in pre-heated oven for 45 minutes. When cool, beat together cream cheese, icing sugar and coffee essence. Spread over top of cake and sprinkle with toasted mixed nuts.

Syrup and Stem Ginger Cake

1 teaspoon (5ml) bicarbonate of soda
5 fl oz (125ml) milk
4 oz (100g) soft margarine
6 tablespoons (90ml) golden syrup
8 oz (200g) plain flour
1 teaspoon (5ml) mixed spice
2 eggs, beaten
2 tablespoons (30ml) soft brown sugar
8 pieces stem ginger, chopped
1 tablespoon (15ml) preserving sugar

Pre-heat oven to 160°C/325°F/Gas 3. Dissolve bicarbonate of soda in milk. Beat all ingredients together except preserving sugar and spoon into a greased, lined 2 lb (800g) loaf tin. Sprinkle with preserving sugar. Bake in pre-heated oven for 1 hour.

Orange Syrup Cake

I first had this cake when visiting our friend, Mandy. Of course, time being of the essence, she was still baking the cake when I arrived. However we proved that it could be eaten warm with the syrup poured over it. In fact it was so good that we ate half of it before I left!

8 oz (200g) soft margarine
8 oz (200g) caster sugar
4 eggs, beaten
2 tablespoons (30ml) ground rice
8 oz (200g) plain flour
2 tablespoons (30ml) baking powder
grated rind of 2 oranges
5 fl oz (125ml) fresh orange juice
3 oz (75g) icing sugar

Pre-heat oven to 180°C/350°F/Gas 4. Beat together all ingredients except orange juice and icing sugar. Spoon the mixture into a greased, lined 2 lb (800g) loaf tin. Bake in pre-heated oven for 75 minutes. Heat the orange juice with the icing sugar in a small pan. Pierce the cake in several places with a sharp skewer, slowly pour the syrup over the cake until it is absorbed by the cake. Leave the cake in the tin overnight, before removing and serving.

Queen Cakes

  4 oz (100g) soft margarine or butter
  4 oz (100g) caster sugar
  4 oz (100g) self-raising flour
  2 eggs, beaten
  2 oz (50g) sultanas

Pre-heat oven to 190°C/375°F/Gas 5. Beat all ingredients together. Spread 12 paper cases on a baking tray and divide mixture between them. Bake in pre-heated oven for 15–20 minutes until golden brown.

  You can adjust this recipe in a number of ways. The following should give you some ideas.

CHOCOLATE CHIP CAKES
Substitute 2 oz (50g) chocolate chips for the sultanas.

COCONUT CAKES
Substitute 2 oz (50g) coconut for the sultanas.

SMARTIE CAKES
Make as for queen cakes but without the sultanas, then sift 3 oz (75g) icing sugar into a bowl and mix in 1 tablespoon (15ml) warm water. Spoon icing onto cakes and press a Smartie on the top of each cake. Leave until icing sets.

Rice Cake

  5 oz (125g) self-raising flour
  3 oz (75g) ground rice
  4 oz (100g) caster sugar
  4 oz (100g) soft margarine or butter
  2 eggs, beaten
  4 tablespoons (60ml) milk
  few drops of almond essence

Pre-heat oven to 180°C/350°F/Gas 4. Beat all ingredients together. Line a 1 lb (400g) loaf tin and spoon mixture in. Bake in pre-heated oven for 60–70 minutes until a skewer inserted into cake's centre comes out clean.

Marmalade Cake

8 oz (200g) self-raising flour
4 oz (100g) caster sugar
4 oz (100g) soft margarine or butter
4 oz (100g) marmalade
2 eggs, beaten
4 tablespoons (60ml) milk

Pre-heat oven to 180°C/350°F/Gas 4. Beat all ingredients together and spoon into a lined 1lb (400g) loaf tin. Cook in pre-heated oven for 60–70 minutes until a skewer placed into cake's centre comes out clean.

Carrot Cake

8 oz (200g) wholemeal flour
1 teaspoon (5ml) ground ginger
1 teaspoon (5ml) nutmeg
1 teaspoon (5ml) baking powder
4 oz (100g) soft margarine or butter
4 oz (100g) brown sugar
4 oz (100g) runny honey
8 oz (200g) carrots, peeled and grated

Pre-heat oven to 180°C/350°F/Gas 4. Beat together all ingredients except honey and carrots, then stir these in. Spoon into a lined 1 lb (400g) loaf tin. Bake in pre-heated oven for 60–70 minutes until a skewer put into the cake's centre comes out clean. The cake can be decorated with orange icing if you wish – just mix 3 oz (75g) sifted icing sugar with 1 tablespoon (15ml) warm orange juice and then spoon over top of cake.

Passion Cake

- 8 oz (200g) soft margarine
- 8 oz (200g) soft brown sugar
- 4 eggs, beaten
- 8 oz (200g) wholemeal self-raising flour
- 1 teaspoon (5ml) baking powder
- 12 oz (300g) carrots, peeled and grated
- grated rind of 1 lemon and 1 tablespoon (15ml) juice
- 4 oz (100g) chopped walnuts
- 3 oz (75g) cream cheese
- 2 oz (50g) icing sugar
- grated rind of 1 orange and juice

Pre-heat oven to 180°C/350°F/Gas 4. Beat together the margarine, sugar, eggs, flour, baking powder, carrots, lemon rind and juice and walnuts. Put in a greased and lined 8 in (20cm) deep cake tin. Bake in pre-heated oven for 90 minutes until well risen and golden brown. When cool, beat together the cream cheese and icing sugar with enough of the orange juice to make a creamy consistency and cover cake top. Sprinkle with grated orange rind.

Walnut Cake

3 eggs, separated
3 oz (75g) soft brown sugar
1 oz (25g) butter
4 oz (100g) mixture of ground and chopped walnuts
2 teaspoons (10ml) coffee essence
sprinkling of icing sugar

Pre-heat oven to 180°C/350°F/Gas 4. Beat egg yolks with sugar for 5 minutes until pale and creamy. Melt butter and add with walnuts and coffee essence to egg mixture. Whisk egg whites until they form soft peaks and gently mix into mixture. Put into a greased, lined 8 in (20cm) flan tin. Bake in pre-heated oven for 30 minutes. Turn out of tin very gently, leave to cool. Sprinkle with icing sugar before serving.

Pecan Pie

12 oz (300g) shortcrust pastry (see p 12)
3 eggs, beaten
1 tablespoon (15ml) single cream
6 oz (150g) soft brown sugar
5 fl oz (125ml) maple syrup
2 oz (50g) soft margarine
1 teaspoon (5ml) vanilla essence
6 oz (150g) pecan nuts, halved

Pre-heat oven to 220°C/425°F/Gas 7. Roll out the pastry to fit an 8 in (20cm) flan tin. Beat all ingredients except nuts together. Put half of nuts into flan case and spoon filling over. Place rest of nuts on top. Bake in pre-heated oven for 10 minutes. Reduce heat to 160°C/325°F/Gas 3 and cook for a further 45 minutes.

Gingerbread

1 tablespoon (15ml) golden syrup
6 tablespoons (90ml) black treacle
3 tablespoons (45ml) molasses sugar
4 oz (100g) soft margarine
8 oz (200g) plain brown flour
2 teaspoons (10ml) baking powder
1 teaspoon (5ml) ground ginger
pinch of mixed spice
2 eggs, beaten
½ teaspoon (3ml) bicarbonate of soda
5 fl oz (125ml) milk

Pre-heat oven to 160°C/325°F/Gas 3. Melt syrup, treacle, sugar and margarine together. Mix in all dry ingredients except bicarbonate of soda. Beat in eggs. Dissolve bicarbonate of soda in milk and add to mixture. Stir well. Put in a greased, lined 2 lb (800g) loaf tin. Bake in pre-heated oven for 90 minutes. If wrapped in foil when cool and kept, it goes lovely and sticky!

Flapjacks

4 oz (100g) soft margarine
4 tablespoons (60ml) golden syrup
1 tablespoon (15ml) soft brown sugar
1 tablespoon (15ml) raisins
8 oz (200g) muesli
4 oz (100g) oats

Pre-heat oven to 150°C/300°F/Gas 2. Melt margarine, syrup and sugar. Mix in all other ingredients. Put in a greased and lined 11×7 in (285×18cm) baking tin. Bake in pre-heated oven for 45 minutes. Divide into 12.

Pumpkin Pie

12 oz (300g) shortcrust pastry (see p 12)
1 lb (400g) pumpkin, cubed
milk
2 eggs, separated
1 tablespoon (15ml) golden syrup
1 teaspoon (5ml) ground ginger
1 teaspoon (5ml) cinnamon
sprinkling of nutmeg

Pre-heat oven to 190°C/375°F/Gas 5. Cook the pumpkin in a little milk until tender (approximately 15 minutes). Remove pumpkin from milk and purée. Roll out the pastry to fit an 8 in (20cm) flan dish. Beat together all ingredients except egg whites and nutmeg. Beat egg whites until stiff and fold into the mixture, spoon into the pastry case and sprinkle with a little nutmeg. Bake in pre-heated oven for 30 minutes.

Treacle Tart

12 oz (300g) shortcrust pastry (see p 12)
5 tablespoons (75ml) golden syrup
1 tablespoon (15ml) black treacle
2 oz (50g) ground almonds
3 oz (75g) fresh white breadcrumbs
grated rind of 1 lemon and 1 tablespoon (15ml) juice
1 egg, beaten
3 tablespoons (45ml) double cream

Pre-heat oven to 190°C/375°F/Gas 5. Roll out pastry to fit a 8 in (20cm) flan tin. Beat rest of ingredients together and pour into pastry case. Bake in pre-heated oven for 30 minutes.

Chocolate Brownies

I don't know how long these will keep in a cake tin – because every time I make them they get eaten immediately!

6 oz (150g) plain chocolate, melted
4 oz (100g) soft margarine
8 oz (200g) soft brown sugar
1 teaspoon (5ml) vanilla essence
2 eggs, beaten
6 oz (150g) wholemeal plain flour
4 oz (100g) raisins
2 oz (50g) nuts, chopped

Pre-heat oven to 180°C/350°F/Gas 4. Beat all ingredients together. Spoon into a greased, lined 11 × 7 in (28 × 8 cm) baking tin. Bake in pre-heated oven for 30 minutes.

Cherry and Almond Loaf

6 oz (150g) soft margarine
6 oz (150g) caster sugar
4 oz (100g) self-raising flour
3 oz (75g) ground almonds
3 eggs, beaten
8 oz (200g) mixed glacé cherries, washed and halved
2 tablespoons (30ml) milk
1 tablespoon (15ml) preserving sugar

Pre-heat oven to 160°C/325°F/Gas 3. Beat together the margarine, caster sugar, flour, ground almonds and eggs. Stir in the glacé cherries and milk (make sure that the cherries are completely dry before adding or they will sink to the bottom of the cake). Put into a greased, lined 2 lb (800g) loaf tin. Sprinkle preserving sugar on top. Bake in pre-heated oven for 50–60 minutes until risen and brown on top.

Marmalade Lattice Tart

1 lb (400g) shortcrust pastry (see p 12)
4 oz (100g) Seville marmalade
4 oz (100g) double cream
2 oz (50g) ground almonds
1 egg, beaten
milk, to glaze
1 tablespoon (15ml) preserving sugar

Pre-heat oven to 190°C/375°F/Gas 5. Roll out two thirds of pastry to fit an 8 in (20cm) flan dish. Place a sheet of greaseproof paper and some coins in it and bake for 15 minutes. Remove paper and coins. Mix together the marmalade, cream, almonds and egg, spoon into pastry case. Roll out rest of pastry to a rectangle 8×4 inch (20×10cm) and cut lengthways into 8 strips. Place 4 strips at equal distances across tart filling. Over these place the other 4 strips at an angle. Glaze with milk and sprinkle with preserving sugar. Bake for a further 20 minutes.

Raisin Slices

4 oz (100g) soft margarine
4 oz (100g) soft brown sugar
3 eggs, beaten
6 oz (150g) wholemeal self-raising flour
4 oz (100g) raisins
1 teaspoon (5ml) ground cinnamon
2 tablespoons (30ml) preserving sugar

Pre-heat oven to 180°C/350°F/Gas 4. Beat all ingredients together except preserving sugar. Spoon into a greased, lined 11×7 in (28×18cm) baking tin. Sprinkle with preserving sugar. Bake in pre-heated oven for 35 minutes. Cut into 15 slices.

Rock Cakes
Makes 8–12

You can also use this recipe to make **Ginger Cakes** by substituting 2 oz (50g) chopped stoned dates and 2 oz (50) chopped stem ginger for the mixed dried fruit.

> 8 oz (200g) wholemeal flour
> ½ teaspoon (2.5g) mixed spice
> 4 oz (100g) soft margarine or butter
> grated rind of half a lemon
> 4 oz (100g) demerara sugar
> 4 oz (100g) mixed dried fruit
> 1 egg, beaten
> 1 tablespoon (15ml) milk

Pre-heat oven to 200°C/400°F/Gas 6. Mix the flour, spice and margarine or butter with an electric mixer. Stir in other ingredients. Place in heaps on a greased baking tray. Bake in pre-heated oven for 15–20 minutes until brown.

Banoffee Pie

> 10 oz (250g) butter, melted
> 8 oz (200g) ginger biscuits, crumbled
> 16-oz (400-g) can condensed milk
> 2 bananas, sliced

Mix 4 oz (100g) butter and biscuits together, line a 7 in (17cm) flan tin with foil and then press biscuit mixture into base of tin. Put rest of butter and condensed milk into a pan, bring to boil and simmer for 5 minutes, leave to cool. Put half of bananas in flan case. When toffee mixture has cooled, beat well and spread over banana. Place remaining banana on top and chill. Serve with cream.

Sweet Nut Flan

12 oz (300g) nutty pastry (see p 12)
1 egg, beaten
1 oz (25g) brown sugar
5 tablespoons (75ml) maple syrup
1 oz (25g) butter, melted
grated rind of half an orange
pinch of cinnamon
1 oz (25g) plain flour
12 oz (300g) mixed whole nuts

Pre-heat oven to 190°C/375°F/Gas 5. Use pastry to line an 8 in (20cm) flan tin, prick pastry base with fork, place grease-proof paper inside flan and weigh down with coins. Bake in pre-heated oven for 15 minutes. Remove paper and coins. Beat together the egg and sugar until thick, add 2 tablespoons (30ml) of the syrup and all other ingredients. Place in flan and bake for 25 minutes. Brush with remaining syrup. Serve hot or cold.

Custard Tart

12 oz (300g) shortcrust pastry (see p 12)
10 fl oz (250ml) milk
2 tablespoons (30ml) caster sugar
3 eggs, beaten
1 tablespoon (15ml) cream
sprinkling of nutmeg

Pre-heat oven to 190°C/375°F/Gas 5. Use pastry to line an 8 in (20cm) flan tin. Prick pastry base all over with a fork, then line with greaseproof paper and weigh down with coins. Bake in pre-heated oven for 15 minutes. Remove paper and coins. To make custard, bring milk and sugar to the boil, pour on to beaten eggs (beat whilst adding milk), pour mixture back into saucepan and bring back to boil, stirring continuously. Take off heat and stir in cream, pour into flan case and sprinkle with nutmeg. Bake at the same temperature for 15–20 minutes until custard has set and is brown on top.

Cherry Custard Tart

12 oz (300g) nutty pastry (see p 12)
1 oz (25g) butter, melted
1 oz (25g) plain flour
10 fl oz (250ml) single cream
2 eggs, beaten
2 oz (50g) caster sugar
1 lb (400g) dessert cherries, stoned

Pre-heat oven to 190°C/375°F/Gas 5. Use pastry to line an 8 in (20cm) flan case. Prick base all over with a fork, line with greaseproof paper and weigh down with coins. Bake in pre-heated oven for 15 minutes. Put butter in a pan on a low heat, stir in flour and then a little cream, continue to add cream whilst stirring. Bring to boil, then lower heat and cook for 1 minute, stirring continously. Beat in eggs and stir in sugar. Remove paper and coins from flan case and place half of fruit inside. Spoon custard over and then top with remaining fruit. Bake for a further 20 minutes.

Plum and Almond Tart

12 oz (300g) nutty pastry (see p 12)
2 oz (50g) ground almonds
2 oz (50g) fresh breadcrumbs
1 lb (400g) eating plums, halved and stoned
2 tablespoons (30ml) redcurrant jelly

Pre-heat oven to 190°C/375°F/Gas 5. Use pastry to line an 8 in (20cm) flan tin, prick base all over with fork. Cover with greaseproof paper and weigh down with coins. Bake in pre-heated oven for 15 minutes. Remove paper and coins. Combine almonds and breadcrumbs and sprinkle over base of tin. Place plums in flan and bake for a further 35 minutes, Melt redcurrant jelly and use to glaze flan.

8 Storecupboard Cookery

There are times when you just don't get the chance to get to the shops in your lunch break or you were going to do the shopping but found that the hole-in-the-wall machine wasn't working, the banks were closed, or the bank manager would go bananas if you wrote one more cheque! When this happens it is time to see what you have in your storecupboard. If you always buy a few items for your storecupboard when you do have a few extra pennies, it will see you through when funds are low or non-existent!

The type of things I make sure that I never run out of include pasta, olive oil, butter, tinned fish such as tuna and anchovies, black olives, pesto, sun-dried tomatoes in oil, tomato purée, cans of chopped tomatoes, chilli sauce, cans of sweetcorn, Parmesan cheese and, of course, garlic.

Pasta with Sun-dried Tomatoes
Serves 2

> 8 oz (200g) pasta
> 4 sun-dried tomatoes in oil, drained and chopped
> 2 oz (50g) pitted black olives, chopped
> 2 tablespoons (30ml) olive oil

Cook pasta as directed on packet. When cooked, mix in other ingredients and serve immediately.

Pasta Tonnato
Serves 2

> 8 oz (200g) pasta
> 8-oz (200-g) can tuna, drained
> 2 oz (50g) pitted black olives, chopped
> 2 tablespoons (30ml) tomato purée
> knob of butter
> black pepper

Cook pasta as directed on packet. In a small pan, place other ingredients and heat gently. Serve mixed into cooked pasta.

Spaghetti with Hot Tomato Sauce
Serves 2

> 8 oz (200g) spaghetti
> 7-oz (200-g) can chopped tomatoes
> 2 tablespoons (30ml) tomato purée
> 1 tablespoon (30ml) chilli sauce
> pinch of sugar
> sprinkling of Italian herbs

Cook spaghetti as directed on packet. Put all other ingredients in a small pan and bring to boiling point, reduce heat and let simmer until sauce thickens. Serve spooned on to cooked spaghetti.

Mushroom Risotto
Serves 2

½ oz (10g) dried mushrooms
2 teaspoons (10ml) garlic purée
knob of butter
6 oz (150g) Arborio rice
15 fl oz (375ml) stock
sprinkling of Italian herbs
2 tablespoons (30ml) Parmesan cheese
black pepper

Pour boiling water over mushrooms and leave to soak for 30 minutes. Drain, reserving water and chop finely. Fry garlic purée in butter and add rice. Stir. Add some of the stock and simmer until absorbed. Add the mushrooms and reserved water, simmer until absorbed. Add the herbs and some more stock, simmer and keep adding stock until rice is cooked (approximately 20 minutes in all). Serve sprinkled with Parmesan and season with black pepper.

Risotto with Tuna and Olives
Serves 2

Follow recipe above but substitute an 8-oz (200-g) can of tuna and a few pitted olives for mushrooms, and add to dish when adding herbs.

Pizza
Serves 2

> 1 pizza dough (see p 11)
> 1 tomato sauce (see p 10)
> 4 oz (100g) grated cheese (Mozzarella and Cheddar are best)

Roll out pizza dough to form base and prick all over with fork. Spread with tomato sauce and sprinkle with cheese. Top with one of the following and bake at 200°C/400°F/Gas 6 for 25–30 minutes.

TOMATO AND OLIVE
4 sun-dried tomatoes, halved
handful of pitted black olives, halved

TUNA AND ANCHOVY
8-oz (200-g) can tuna, drained
2-oz (50-g) can anchovies, drained

SARDINE AND SWEETCORN
6-oz (150-g) can sardines, drained
8-oz (200-g) can sweetcorn, drained

PINEAPPLE AND SWEETCORN
8-oz (200-g) can pineapple chunks, drained
8-oz (200-g) can sweetcorn, drained
1 tablespoon (15ml) tomato ketchup
1 tablespoon (15ml) soy sauce
Mix all ingredients together and spread over pizza.

HERB AND GARLIC
2 cloves garlic, crushed
1 tablespoon (15ml) olive oil
1 tablespoon (15ml) Italian herbs
Fry garlic in oil until soft, then drizzle over pizza and sprinkle with herbs.

Pan Pizza
Serves 2

6 oz (150g) self-raising flour
1 teaspoon (5ml) salt
4 teaspoons (20ml) oil
oil, for frying
4 tablespoons (60ml) tomato purée
1 tablespoon (15ml) pesto
sprinkling of Parmesan cheese

Mix flour, salt and oil together. Add enough water to make a soft dough (approximately 6 tablespoons/90ml). Knead and press out to fit a frying pan. Fry for 4 minutes over a medium heat, turn and cook other side. Spread with tomato purée and pesto. Sprinkle with Parmesan. Grill for a few minutes under a hot grill.

Frittata
Serves 2

2 tablespoons (30ml) olive oil
3 eggs, beaten
8-oz (200-g) can sweetcorn, drained
handful of pitted black olives, chopped
2 tablespoons (30ml) milk
black pepper

Heat oil in a frying pan whilst mixing all other ingredients. Pour into pan and cook on a medium heat for 5 minutes. Cook for a further few minutes under a medium grill to brown top.

Pasta Frittata
Serves 2

    2 tablespoons (30ml) olive oil
    4 eggs, beaten
    2 oz (50g) cooked pasta
    4-oz (100-g) can tuna, drained
    1 tablespoon (15ml) tomato ketchup
    dash of Tabasco sauce

Heat oil whilst mixing together other ingredients. Pour into oil and cook on a medium heat for 5 minutes, cook for a further few minutes under a medium grill until brown on top.

9 Just Like Mother Used to Make. . .

Like many of today's mothers, my mother has always been a working woman. As she had a long journey to work and a house and children to look after, it is not surprising that she often resorted to simple suppers, such as grilled chops or chicken pieces, to feed us. However, weekends were different and when I think back to my childhood, I always fondly remember casseroles and stews that had been gently cooked for hours and were meltingly tender, and weekend roasts (I still think my mother does the best roast potatoes in the world). As we got older and more cosmopolitan ingredients could be found in the shops, an ethnic air began to creep into our favourite dishes and curry, lasagne and spaghetti bolognese found their way on to our plates. Our tastes are still expanding.

It is not often that one has the time to spend a few hours in the kitchen but it is possible at the weekend. I've collected here some of my family's favourite dishes, although my brother Desmond's favourite, cassoulet, is not here as he is still working on the perfect recipe!

I have also not included recipes for roasts as the best joints are always too large for just two people – I prefer only to do a roast dinner for 6–8 guests. However, if you do have a roast and have some leftover meat, there are some dishes in this chapter which can be made with cooked meat, e.g. chicken fricassee, rissoles, shepherd's pie.

I hope you find some of your forgotten favourites here.

Beef Curry
Serves 4

This was the first curry we ever had, although I have now replaced the curry powder with curry paste. The original recipe (and curry powder) was given to my mother by a West Indian nurse she knew. The coconut milk used here is tinned – and can be also used to make Pina Coladas!

    2 onions, chopped
    2 cloves garlic, crushed
    2 tablespoons (30ml) oil
    1 tablespoon (15ml) curry paste
    pinch of ground ginger
    1 lb (400g) stewing beef, cubed
    15 fl oz (375ml) beef stock
    5 fl oz (125ml) coconut milk

Fry the onion and garlic in oil until brown. Add the curry paste, ginger and meat and stir whilst continuing to fry until meat is brown on all sides. Add the stock, bring to the boil, cover tightly and simmer slowly for 2 hours. Add the coconut milk and warm through. Serve with rice and poppadoms.

Chicken Curry
Serves 2

    1 lb (400g) chicken meat
    2 tablespoons (30ml) flour
    1 tablespoon (15ml) curry powder
    2 oz (50g) butter
    1 tablespoon (15ml) tomato purée
    8 fl oz (200ml) chicken stock

Pre-heat oven to 160°C/325°F/Gas 3. Toss the chicken in the flour and curry powder. Fry in the butter until brown, add the tomato purée and mix well, add the stock and bring to the boil. Transfer to an ovenproof dish. Cover with a tight fitting lid and cook in pre-heated oven for 90 minutes. Serve with rice and poppadoms.

Beef Cobbler
Serves 2

1 onion, chopped
2 tablespoons (30ml) oil
1 green pepper, deseeded and chopped
12 oz (300g) stewing beef, cubed
5 fl oz (125ml) beef stock or red wine
1 tablespoon (15ml) tomato purée
4 oz (100g) self-raising flour
pinch of salt
1 oz (25g) margarine
1 oz (25g) cheese, grated
4 tablespoons (60ml) milk

Pre-heat oven to 180°C/350°F/Gas 4. Fry the onion in oil, transfer to an ovenproof dish. Fry the green pepper and transfer to dish. Fry the beef until brown, add stock or wine and tomato purée. Simmer for 5 minutes and then transfer to dish. Bake in pre-heated oven for 90 minutes. Rub together the flour, salt and margarine. Rub in cheese and then use milk to bind into a dough. Roll out and, using a scone cutter, make scones. Place on surface of casserole, turn heat up to 230°C/450°F/Gas 8 and cook for 10 minutes. Serve with green vegetables or carrots.

Beef in Beer
Serves 2

1 onion, chopped
4 oz (100g) carrots, diced
2 tablespoons (30ml) oil
12 oz (300g) stewing beef, cubed
1 tablespoon (15ml) flour
8 fl oz (200ml) brown ale
1 tablespoon (15ml) tomato purée
sprinkling of mixed herbs

Pre-heat oven to 160°C/325°F/Gas 3. Fry onion and carrot in oil until soft. Transfer to an ovenproof dish. Fry beef until brown. Stir in flour and then slowly add beer. Stir in tomato purée, bring to boil before adding herbs and then transfer to the ovenproof dish. Cover and bake in pre-heated oven for 2 hours. Serve with jacket or mashed potatoes and a green vegetable.

Braised Steak
Serves 2

  2 × 6 oz (2× 150g) rib eye steaks
  1 tablespoon (15ml) oil
  1 onion, thinly sliced
  1 tablespoon (15ml) flour
  knob of butter
  1 tablespoon (15ml) brown sugar
  8 fl oz (200ml) Belgian lager

Pre-heat oven to 180°C/350°F/Gas 4. Fry the steaks in the oil for 1 minute on each side. Transfer to an ovenproof dish. Fry the onion until soft, add the flour, butter and sugar. Stir well, continue to heat while slowly adding lager. Bring to boil before transferring to ovenproof dish. Cover and bake in pre-heated oven for 40 minutes. Serve with new potatoes and a green vegetable.

Chicken and Bacon Casserole
Serves 2

  1 onion, chopped
  2 sticks celery, chopped
  4 oz (100g) streaky bacon, chopped
  1 tablespoon (15ml) oil
  knob of butter
  2 chicken quarters
  1 tablespoon (15ml) flour
  14-oz (400-g) can chopped tomatoes
  black pepper

Pre-heat oven to 180°C/350°F/Gas 4. Fry the onion, celery and bacon in the oil until soft. Transfer to an ovenproof dish. Add the butter to the frying pan and fry the chicken until brown. Stir in the flour and then the tomatoes. Season and transfer to the ovenproof dish. Bake in pre-heated oven for 1 hour. Serve with rice and peas.

Chicken Fricassee
Serves 2

This is a very useful dish for using up roast chicken, but can also be made with chicken slices bought from a delicatessen.

    1 onion, chopped
    1 tablespoon (15ml) oil
    4 oz (100g) mushrooms, sliced
    10 fl oz (250ml) white sauce (see p 9)
    8 oz (200g) cooked chicken, sliced
    1 tablespoon (15ml) cream
    chopped parsley, to garnish

Fry the onion in the oil until soft, add the mushrooms and fry for a further 3 minutes. Stir in the white sauce and chicken, heat through. Stir in the cream. Serve on a bed of rice garnished with parsley, or alternatively, serve with triangles of toast.

Chicken Maryland
Serves 2

4 chicken drumsticks
2 tablespoons (30ml) flour
1 tablespoon (15ml) paprika
1 egg, beaten
dried breadcrumbs
2 tablespoons (30ml) oil
knob of butter
2 bananas

Coat the chicken with flour and paprika. Dip into egg and then roll in dried breadcrumbs. Fry in oil and butter until golden and cooked through. (This should take about 15 minutes on a low heat). Halve bananas, coat in egg and then roll in breadcrumbs. Turn up heat and cook quickly until brown. Serve with sweetcorn. (If you are completely unconcerned about calories, you can make **Sweetcorn Fritters** to serve with this – simply mix sweetcorn with some batter and fry a tablespoon at a time for a few minutes on each side.)

Chicken Pie
Serves 2

10 fl oz (250ml) white sauce (see p 9)
8 oz (200g) cooked chicken, diced
4 oz (100g) cooked vegetables (whatever you have available)
dash of Worcester sauce
1 sheet puff pastry

Pre-heat oven to 220°C/425°F/Gas 7. Mix together the white sauce, chicken and vegetables. Season with Worcester sauce and put in a pie dish. Cover with puff pastry and trim edges. Cut 2 slits in the middle of the pie. Bake in pre-heated oven for 25 minutes. Serve with jacket potatoes.

Chilli Beef Pie
Serves 2

    2 servings Chilli con carne (see p 168)
    1 sheet puff pastry

Pre-heat oven to 220°C/425°F/Gas 7. Put chilli mixture into a pie dish, cover with puff pastry, trim edges. Bake in pre-heated oven for 25 minutes. Serve with a green vegetable.

Cod with Parsley Sauce
Serves 2

    2 cod steaks
    10 fl oz (250ml) parsley sauce (see p 9)

Boil some water in a saucepan. Place steaks in water, cover and simmer gently for 10 minutes. Remove fish from pan and serve with parsley sauce. Good with new potatoes and carrots.

Fish and Chips
Serve 2

Although one can fry fish in breadcrumbs, I prefer to bake mine.

　　2 cod fillets
　　1 egg, beaten
　　dried breadcrumbs
　　1 lb (400g) potatoes, peeled and chipped
　　oil, for frying

Pre-heat oven to 200°C/400°F/Gas 6. Brush fish with egg and then dip fish into breadcrumbs and coat thoroughly. Put on a greased baking tray and bake in pre-heated oven for 25 minutes. Whilst baking, wash chips well and dry with kitchen paper or clean tea towel. Heat oil to 190°C/375°F. (If you are not using a safety fat fryer, this is the temperature when a chip will rise to the surface and start cooking immediately when dropped into the fat.) Lower the chips in, being careful not to overfill basket. Cook for 7–8 minutes until golden and crispy. Drain and serve with fish and perhaps some peas. Good with tomato or tartare sauce.

Fishcakes
Serves 2

　　1 lb (400g) potatoes, mashed
　　8 oz (200g) white or 4oz (100g) oily fish, cooked
　　salt and pepper
　　1 tablespoon (15ml) milk
　　1 egg, beaten
　　dried breadcrumbs
　　oil, for frying

Mix together the mashed potato and fish, season with salt and pepper. Using the milk, bind into a dough. Divide into quarters and shape each portion into a cake. Brush with egg and dip in breadcrumbs to ensure an even coating. Put in a frying pan with a small amount of oil and fry for 3 minutes on each side over a gentle heat. Serve with a green vegetable or a small salad, with tomato sauce or a mayonnaise-based sauce.

Fish Pie
Serves 2

> 8 oz (200g) white fish fillet
> 10 fl oz (250ml) white sauce (see p 9)
> knob of butter
> few fresh chives, chopped
> salt and pepper
> 1 sheet puff pastry
> milk to glaze

Pre-heat oven to 220°C/425°F/Gas 7. Poach fish in a little water until cooked (about 8 minutes). When cooked, flake into sauce and season with salt and pepper, stir in chives. Put into an ovenproof dish and cover with the pastry. Glaze with milk. Bake in pre-heated oven for 25 minutes. Serve with new potatoes and a green vegetable.

Gammon, Pineapple and Chips
Serves 2

> 2 gammon steaks
> 2 rings pineapple, fresh or tinned
> 1 lb (400g) potatoes, peeled and chipped
> oil, for frying

Put gammon steaks under a medium grill for 6 minutes. Whilst cooking fry chips in hot oil (190°C/375°F) (see p 165), they will take about 7–8 minutes. When one side of gammon steaks is done, turn over, place a pineapple ring on each steak and grill for a further 5 minutes. Serve with chips and peas, carrots or sweetcorn.

Goulash
Serves 2

 1 onion, chopped
 1 green pepper, deseeded and chopped
 2 tablespoons (30ml) oil
 12 oz (300g) stewing beef, cubed
 2 tablespoons (30ml) flour
 1 tablespoon (15ml) paprika
 2 tablespoons (30ml) tomato purée
 15 fl oz (375ml) beer

Pre-heat oven to 160°C/325°F/Gas 3. Fry the onion and pepper in oil until browning. Transfer to a casserole dish. Mix beef with flour and paprika, fry on all sides until brown – about 5 minutes. Add tomato purée and beer and bring to the boil. Transfer to the casserole dish. Cover and bake in pre-heated oven for 90 minutes. Serve with rice and carrots.

Ham, Egg and Chips
Serves 2

This is one of our family's all-time favourites. Chips were always a treat and since this dish is also very cheap to make, it is a good way of stretching the budget at the end of the month.

 2 ham steaks
 1 lb (400g) potatoes, peeled and chipped
 2 eggs

Grill ham steaks for about 5 minutes on each side. Fry chips in oil pre-heated to 190°C/375°F for 7–8 minutes (see p 165). Pre-heat a frying pan with a little oil in it and break in eggs. Cook on a medium heat for about 4–5 minutes. Spoon a little hot fat over egg yolk to help cook it. Serve with tomato or brown sauce.

Lamb Stew with Dumplings
Serves 2

    12 oz (300g) stewing lamb, cubed
    1 stewpack of vegetables, peeled and cubed
    oil, for frying
    15 fl oz (375ml) lamb stock
    black pepper
    1 tablespoon (15ml) tomato purée
    4 oz (100g) self-raising flour
    2 oz (50g) shredded suet
    sprinkling of mixed herbs
    little water

Pre-heat oven to 160°C/325°F/Gas 3. Fry lamb until brown on all sides and transfer to a casserole dish. Quickly fry vegetables until browning and add to dish. Season with pepper and mix in stock and tomato purée. Cover and bake in pre-heated oven for 1 hour. Blend together the flour, suet, herbs and enough of the water to make a dough. Divide into 8 portions and roll each into a ball. Place on top of the meat and vegetables, cover and cook for 20 minutes. This is a complete meal in itself, but you may like to serve wholemeal bread with which to soak up the gravy.

Chilli con Carne
Serves 4

    1 onion, chopped
    1 clove garlic, crushed
    1 green pepper, deseeded and chopped
    2 tablespoons (30ml) oil
    1 lb (400g) minced beef
    2 tablespoons (30ml) tomato purée
    14-oz (400-g) can chopped tomatoes
    1 packet chilli mix
    16-oz (400-g) can red kidney beans, drained

Fry the onion, garlic and pepper in oil until soft. Add mince and continue to cook until brown. Add the rest of ingredients and mix well. Cover tightly and simmer gently for 1 hour. Serve with rice.

Lasagne
Serves 2

1 onion, chopped
1 clove garlic, crushed
1 red pepper, deseeded and chopped
2 tablespoons (30ml) olive oil
8 oz (200g) minced beef
1 tablespoon (15ml) tomato purée
14-oz (400-g) can chopped tomatoes
sprinkling of Italian herbs
4 sheets no-cook lasagne
10 fl oz (250ml) cheese sauce (see p 9)
sprinkling of Parmesan cheese

Pre-heat oven to 180°C/350°F/Gas 4. Fry onion, garlic and pepper in oil. Add mince and fry until brown. Add tomato purée, tomatoes and herbs. Simmer gently for 15 minutes. Place a layer of meat sauce in a greased ovenproof dish. Cover with lasagne and then some cheese sauce. Continue to layer the meat sauce, then lasagne, then cheese sauce. Finish with a layer of cheese sauce. Sprinkle with Parmesan cheese and bake in pre-heated oven for 35 minutes until golden brown on top. Serve with garlic bread and a tomato or green salad.

Lancashire Hot-pot
Serves 2

4 lamb chops
1 onion, sliced
1 carrot, sliced
10 fl oz (250ml) lamb stock
dash of Worcester sauce
8 oz (200g) potatoes, peeled and thinly sliced
knob of butter

Pre-heat oven to 160°C/325°F/Gas 3. Put all ingredients except potatoes and butter in a casserole dish. Cover with sliced potatoes and dot with butter. Cover, cook in pre-heated oven for 90 minutes, remove cover and turn heat up to 220°C/425°F/Gas 7 for 20 minutes. Serve with carrots.

Liver and Onions
Serves 2

    2 onions, sliced
    2 tablespoons (30ml) oil
    knob of butter
    sprinkling of brown sugar
    sprinkling of mixed herbs
    8 oz (200g) lambs' liver, thinly sliced
    2 tablespoons (30ml) lamb stock

Fry the onions in the oil and butter until starting to colour. Add the sugar and herbs, cover and simmer gently for 10 minutes. Add the liver, increase the heat slightly and fry on both sides. Add the stock, cover and cook for 8 minutes until liver is cooked through. Serve with mashed potatoes and peas or carrots.

Moussaka
Serves 2

1 aubergine, sliced
2 tablespoons (30ml) olive oil
1 onion, chopped
1 clove garlic, crushed
8 oz (200g) minced lamb
sprinkling of oregano
14-oz (400g) can chopped tomatoes
2 tablespoons (30ml) tomato purée
1 egg, beaten
5 fl oz (125ml) Greek yoghurt
3 oz (75g) cheese, grated

Pre-heat oven to 200°C/400°F/Gas 6. Fry the aubergine in half of the oil, put aside. Fry onion and garlic in remaining oil until soft, add minced lamb and brown. Add oregano, tomatoes and tomato purée. Put a layer of meat sauce into a greased ovenproof dish, add a layer of aubergine, continue with layers, finishing with a layer of aubergine. Mix together the egg, yoghurt and cheese. Spoon over aubergine. Bake in pre-heated oven for 30 minutes. Serve with garlic bread and a tomato or green salad.

Macaroni Cheese
Serves 2

4 oz (100g) quick-cook macaroni
10 fl oz (250ml) cheese sauce (see p 9)
knob of butter
1 teaspoon (5ml) French mustard
sprinkling of fresh breadcrumbs
1 oz (25g) Cheddar, grated
dash of Worcester sauce

Pre-heat oven to 200°C/400°F/Gas 6. Cook macaroni as directed on packet, drain. Mix with cheese sauce, butter and mustard. Transfer to an ovenproof dish. Cover with bread-crumbs and grated cheese. Top with a dash of Worcester sauce. Bake in pre-heated oven for 20 minutes. Serve with a tomato salad and garlic bread.

Pork and Apple in Cider
Serves 2

    1 onion, chopped
    1 tablespoon (15ml) oil
    knob of butter
    1 large cooking apple, peeled, cored and sliced
    2 pork chops, fat removed
    10 fl oz (250ml) cider
    sprinkling of sage

Pre-heat oven to 160°C/325°F/Gas 3. Fry the onion in the oil and butter until golden. Put into a greased ovenproof dish with the apple slices and place chops on top. Pour over cider and sprinkle with sage. Cover tightly and cook in pre-heated oven for 90 minutes. Serve with a green vegetable and new potatoes.

Spaghetti Bolognese
Serves 2

    1 onion, chopped
    1 clove garlic, crushed
    1 tablespoon (15ml) oil
    8 oz (200g) minced beef
    2 oz (50g) mushrooms, sliced
    2 tablespoons (30ml) tomato purée
    1 tablespoon (15ml) pesto
    black pepper
    5 oz (125g) spaghetti

Fry the onion and garlic in the oil until soft. Add minced beef and fry until brown. Add mushrooms and cook for a further minute. Stir in tomato purée, pesto and pepper. Simmer gently (adding a little water or wine if sauce is too thick) for 10 minutes. Cook spaghetti as directed on packet. Serve with Parmesan cheese and garlic bread.

Shepherd's Pie
Serves 2

1 onion, chopped
1 carrot, chopped
2 tablespoons (30ml) oil
8 oz cooked meat, minced
1 tablespoon (15ml) tomato purée
sprinkling of parsley
salt and pepper
dash of Worcester sauce
5 fl oz (125ml) brown stock
1 lb (400g) cooked potato, mashed
knob of butter

Pre-heat oven to 190°C/375°F/Gas 5. Fry onion and carrot in oil until soft. Add minced meat, tomato purée, parsley, salt and pepper, Worcester sauce and stock. Cook until stock is reduced by half. Put into a greased ovenproof dish. Mix butter and potato together and use to cover mince. Bake in pre-heated oven until potato is brown. Serve with peas.

Steak and Kidney Pie
Serves 2

1 onion, chopped
1 tablespoon (15ml) oil
1 tablespoon (15ml) flour
12 oz (300g) steak and kidney mix, cubed
15 fl oz (375ml) beef stock
salt and pepper
1 sheet puff pastry
milk, to glaze

Pre-heat oven to 220°C/425°F/Gas 7. Fry onion in oil until soft. Mix flour with the steak and kidney, add to onion and fry until brown. Add stock, cover and continue to cook for 1 hour. Season and transfer to a pie dish. Cover with the puff pastry, trim edges and glaze with milk. Bake in pre-heated oven for 25 minutes. Serve with carrots and new potatoes.

Toad in the Hole
Serves 2

8 oz (200g) sausages
5 fl oz (125ml) batter (see p 11)

Pre-heat oven to 220°C/425°F/Gas 7. Put sausages into a greased deep baking tin. Pour in batter and cook in pre-heated oven for 30–40 minutes until brown. Serve with mashed potato and baked beans.

Cheese on Toast
Serves 2

> 4 oz (100g) cheese, grated
> pinch of dry mustard
> dash of Worcester sauce
> salt and pepper
> milk
> 4 slices bread

Season the cheese with mustard, Worcester sauce and salt and pepper, and mix to a paste with some milk. Toast the bread on one side and then turn over and cover other side with cheese paste (take cheese right up to sides of bread), grill until brown and bubbling. This is an all-time favourite of mine!

Here are two variations on cheese on toast that you may like to try.

WELSH RAREBIT
Serves 2

> 4 oz (100g) cheese, grated
> knob of butter
> pinch of dry mustard
> 2 tablespoons (30ml) beer (or cider or milk)
> salt and pepper
> 4 slices bread

Put all ingredients except bread in a small saucepan and heat gently until they melt. Toast bread on one side. Turn over and spoon mixture on to toast. Grill until brown and bubbling.

FRIED CHEESE AND BACON SANDWICH
Serves 2

> 4 slices streaky bacon
> 4 slices bread
> knob of butter
> 4 slices Gruyère cheese

Fry bacon without added fat until crispy, remove from pan and crumble. Fry bread in butter on one side only. Remove 2 slices from pan and keep warm. Place 2 slices Gruyère on each fried side of bread, cover the frying pan and fry until cheese melts. Serve with bacon crumbled into cheese and topped with other pieces of bread (fried side uppermost).

Beefburgers
Serves 2

8 oz (200g) minced beef
salt and pepper
1 tablespoon (15ml) oil

Divide beef into 4 equal amounts and season. Shape each portion into a flat round cake. Cook in the oil over a medium heat for 5 minutes, turning once. Serve in baps or with salad and chips.

Curried Mince
Serves 2

1 onion, chopped
1 pepper, deseeded and chopped
1 tablespoon (15ml) oil
8 oz (200g) minced beef
2 teaspoons (10ml) curry powder
6 fl oz (150ml) beef stock
sprinkling of sultanas
1 tablespoon (15ml) mango chutney

Fry onion and pepper in oil until soft. Add mince and fry until brown, sprinkle in curry powder and stir in. Pour in stock and bring to boil, add sultanas, cover tightly and simmer gently until stock reduces and mince is cooked (about 15–20 minutes). Stir in mango chutney and serve on jacket potatoes or with rice and poppadoms.

Swedish Salad
Serves 2

1 apple, cored and sliced
1 banana, sliced
lemon juice
5 fl oz (125ml) double cream, lightly whipped
3 tablespoons (45ml) mayonnaise
1 teaspoon (5ml) curry powder
1 tablespoon (15ml) mango chutney
2 cooked chicken quarters, boned and shredded

Sprinkle fruit with lemon juice. Mix together cream, mayonnaise and curry powder, and mix with all ingredients. Serve with a rice salad and a green salad.

Mixed Grill
Serves 2

2 tomatoes, halved
4 medium mushrooms
salt and pepper
2 lamb chops
4 chipolata sausages
2 rashers back bacon
melted butter

Heat grill to a medium heat. Put tomatoes (cut side up) and mushrooms (stalk side up) in the bottom of the grill pan, season. Put chops and bacon on grill rack, brush with butter and season. Grill for 10 minutes, turning frequently. Add bacon and grill for another 5 minutes until all meat is cooked. Serve with chips or baked beans and fried egg.

Sardines on Toast
Serves 2

4-oz (100-g) can sardines in tomato sauce
dash of Worcester sauce
sprinkling of lemon juice
2 tablespoons (30ml) fresh breadcrumbs
4 slices bread
soft margarine or butter
sprinkling of chopped fresh parsley

Mash together sardines, Worcester sauce, lemon juice and breadcrumbs. Toast one side of bread and turn over, thickly butter and cover with sardine mixture. Grill until brown and crisping. Serve sprinkled with parsley.

Ratatouille
Serves 4

2 tablespoons (30ml) olive oil
2 tablespoons (30ml) soft margarine or butter
1 aubergine, cubed
4 courgettes, cubed
8 oz (200g) mushrooms, quartered
1 onion, chopped
2 cloves garlic, crushed
2 tablespoons (30ml) chopped fresh parsley
2 × 14-oz (2 × 400-g) can chopped tomatoes
1 tablespoon (15ml) tomato purée
salt and pepper

Pre-heat oven to 180°C/350°F/Gas 4. Heat oil and butter and quickly stir-fry vegetables, season, put into an ovenproof dish and cover tightly. Cook in pre-heated oven for 60 minutes. Serve with rice or pasta. Can also be served with garlic bread, sour cream and grated cheese.

Ratpie
Serves 2

2 portions ratatouille
sprinkling of herbes de Provence
2 oz (50g) cheese, grated
12 oz (300g) cheese or nutty pastry (see p 12)
sesame seeds
milk, to glaze

Pre-heat oven to 200°C/400°F/Gas 6. Put ratatouille into a pie dish and mix in herbs, sprinkle with cheese and then cover with pastry (use any extra pastry to decorate). Make two slits in top of pastry, brush with milk and sprinkle with sesame seeds. Bake in pre-heated oven for 35 minutes until pastry is brown and cooked. Serve with salad or broccoli.

Salad Niçoise
Serves 2

4 tomatoes, sliced
half a cucumber, sliced
4 oz (100g) French beans, cooked
2-oz (50-g) can anchovies, drained
sprinkling of olives
sprinkling of chopped fresh parsley
French or garlic dressing

Mix all ingredients together and serve immediately. I like to serve this with hard boiled eggs, sun-dried tomatoes and baby potatoes or garlic bread.

Barbecued Spare Ribs
Serves 2

We are very keen on barbecued anything in our family and one of my mother's standbys is this recipe which she always makes with spare rib chops. I have used spare ribs here as they are readily available in most supermarkets.

   1 lb (400g) spare ribs
   4 tablespoons (60ml) tomato ketchup
   2 tablespoons (30ml) orange juice
   1 tablespoon (15ml) soy sauce
   1 tablespoon (15ml) runny honey
   2 cloves garlic, crushed
   black pepper

Pre-heat oven to 190°C/375°F/Gas 5. Mix all ingredients together and marinate for 4–24 hours in the fridge. Place in a baking dish and cook in the pre-heated oven for 60 minutes. Turn during baking and baste with marinade. Serve with baked potatoes or garlic bread and salad. If you enjoy spicy food you can make **Chilli Ribs** by replacing the tomato ketchup, orange juice and soy sauce with 5 fl oz (125ml) beer and adding a pinch of dry mustard and 1 tablespoon (15ml) chilli sauce. Cook as above.

Lamb in Red Wine
Serves 4

2 lb (800g) lean stewing lamb, cubed
2 oz (50g) butter
2 onions, chopped
4 rashers streaky bacon, chopped
2 cloves garlic, crushed
1 tablespoon (15ml) flour
half a bottle of red wine
5 fl oz (125ml) orange juice
sprinkling of rosemary
salt and pepper

Pre-heat oven to 180°C/350°F/Gas 4. Fry lamb in butter until brown and remove to an ovenproof dish. Fry onion, bacon and garlic for 5 minutes, stir in flour and cook for 1 minute. Add to lamb with all other ingredients. Cover and cook in pre-heated oven for 2 hours. Serve with new potatoes and carrots.

Lamb Boulangère
Serves 2

2 portions lamb in red wine (see above)
8 oz (200g) potato, sliced
salt and pepper
melted butter

Pre-heat oven to 200°C/400°F/Gas 6. Put lamb in a pie dish. Boil potato for 5 minutes. Cover lamb with overlapping slices of potato and season. Brush with melted butter. Cook in pre-heated oven for 30 minutes until potato is golden and crispy. Serve with peas.

Index

chops: Chinese, grilled 53
  honey and ginger glazed 19
  see also pork chops
chow mein
  chicken and mushroom 21
  chicken and pineapple 108
cod: in American sauce 82
  and bacon casserole 95
  in coriander sauce 98
  curried 79
  with parsley sauce 164
  in red mayonnaise sauce 64
  steaks with blue cheese 20
coley with spicy sauce 22
country cake 137
courgette and nut roast 52
courgettes 120
  and mushrooms, with pasta 73
  stuffed 34
curried cod 79
curried egg salad 57
curried mince 176
curries: beef 159
  chicken 159
  chickpea and coriander 19
  pork and pineapple 84
  Thai okra and peanut 23
  Thai pork 93
custard tart 149

desserts 129-50
dumplings 168

economy 2
egg and bacon salad 41
egg salad, curried 57
eggs: Florentine 86
  tuna-stuffed 59

fennel 120
fish: bake (frozen fish) 15
  balls, in tomato sauce 113
  and chips 165
  creole 68
  crispy cheesy 44
  with ginger 82
  with lemon sauce 42
  in mushroom sauce 80
  pie 166
  steaks, pan-fried 43
  Tikka fillets 56
fishcakes 165
  tuna 72
flapjacks 144

French beans 121
frittata 155
  pork and prawn 27
  pasta 156
fruit 129-50

gammon steaks: fruity 67
  glazed 22
  with pineapple and chips 166
garlic bread 10
gingerbread 144
gnocchi with mozzarella and basil, baked 104
goulash 167
gravy 8
Greek lamb 53
  kebabs 48

haddock: mornay 109
  smoked, gratin 74
ham and cheese fry-up 18
ham and courgette gratin 43
ham and pasta bake 47
ham, egg and chips 167
herring: fried mustardy 50
  stuffed 21
honey cake 132
honeyed chicken 14
hot-pot, Lancashire 169

Indonesian chicken salad 52

Jerusalem artichokes 121

kebabs: chicken and banana 83
  gingery coconut chicken 48
  Greek lamb 48
  turkey and avocado 114
  vegetable 57
kedgeree 99
kidneys, devilled 102
kippers with orange butter 98
kitchen equipment 4-5

lamb
  boulangère 181
  and broccoli 77
  couscous 67
  fruity pilau 54
  hash 79
  with mint jelly 76
  with mint mustard 56
  in mustard and rosemary sauce 92
  in orange sauce 54
  and pepper stir-fry 55
  peppery, in orange sauce 72